MW01280003

Stop Drinking And Get Fit

Copyright © 2013 by Fred Krueger.

All rights reserved. No part of this publication may be reproduced, distributed or transmitted in any form or by any means, including photocopying, recording, or other electronic or mechanical methods, without the prior written permission of the publisher, except in the case of brief quotations embodied in critical reviews and certain other noncommercial uses permitted by copyright law. For permission requests, write to the publisher, "Attention: Permissions Coordinator," at the address below.

Fred Krueger
3100 Donald Douglas Loop North, #7
Santa Monica, CA 90405

Stop Drinking And Get Fit!/Fred Krueger —1st edition.
ISBN 978-1-496-19462-6

Dedicated to my dog, Alaska,
and to the number
$e = 2.718.$

"Stopping drinking is easy. All you have do is change ... everything."

rHeard in many AA meetings...

[1]

Introduction

I WANT YOU TO STOP DRINKING. Whether you are a middle-aged woman hooked on chardonnay, a twenty-year-old single-malt aficionado, a successful businessman with a taste for fine wine, or a construction worker who likes to kick back with a couple of "brewskies" after work, I can promise you that your life will be significantly better, richer and more rewarding if you completely, absolutely, kick the alcohol habit.

I am not talking about "cutting back", or reducing your intake to a glass a day. I am not talking about substituting pot for alcohol. What I am suggesting is a radical, complete transformation where you quit *all forms of* alcohol, street drugs and painkillers – full stop.

If this doesn't sound impossible enough, I want you to lose a *lot* of weight. If you are an average adult male with a height of 5' 10", I want you to get down to 160 pounds. If you are an average adult female around 5' 4", I want to see you weigh in at 120 pounds. In terms of body fat, I want to see you in the lean zone. For a 53-year-old man like myself, that means 17% or less. If you are a 25-year-old guy, you should be very close to the single digits.

If this sounds preposterous, keep reading. *I did exactly what I am recommending over a six-month period.* I speak from direct, personal, experience. Before I started the program, I was pushing 198 pounds and was at 27% body fat. Clinically, this is considered obese. I had a long history of drinking – typically a bottle of wine per day, *every* day. Today, I weigh 159 pounds, have 16% body fat, and don't even *think* about drinking.

The reason I am writing this book is to communicate to you that this kind of transformation is possible in each and every one of us. It may not even take six months. In just 90 days, you can completely change you who are -- physically, mentally, emotionally.

It won't be easy, but it also won't be anywhere near as difficult as you might imagine. As with a lot of things in life, sometimes making *big* changes is easier than making *small* ones. The key is to commit to a *total* lifestyle change. "Moderation" is not your friend.

There is a saying that goes, "If you don't know where you are going, any road will take you there."

Most people just go through life trying to "drink socially" and "eat reasonably" without any clear idea of what "socially" or "reasonably" even means. As a result, 70% of Americans are overweight, 10% have a severe alcohol problem, and almost everybody is unhappy with their physical appearance.

If this book makes you even begin to *suspect* that alcohol is making your life worse, not better, it will have been worth writing. But even more importantly, I want to bring to you a very positive message about how great your life can be *without* alcohol or drugs. As a drinker, I am sure you are thinking, "How drab and boring would that be?" *I* certainly did. And I was completely wrong.

Drinking, like fast food and corn syrup, has ingrained itself into modern society and the modern lifestyle like a virus. It's a mass problem without an easy solution. But you as an individual can choose to rise above this problem and choose a life of clarity and sobriety. I want to show you how to do it, and why this lifestyle is desirable.

There are huge collateral advantages. My blood pressure, which was off the charts, is now normal, without any medication. My sex drive is healthy – no need for the "purple pill" that so many people my age rely on (and that I used to believe was necessary). My cholesterol and other blood indicators have gone from "disturbing" to "perfect". At 53, I am in better shape than I was in college. And you can be too.

My mind's capabilities have exploded. In just a few months of sobriety, I learned to play basic piano. I read voraciously, sleep well, and am generally very happy. Without drinking, I have much time to sit and think about things, to organize my life and explore all kinds of subjects I kept putting off. I am not saying this to brag; I am saying it to inspire you. You too will experience these types of everyday miracles.

As a drinker, one often "checks out" around 7pm at night. It's all about "vegging out" in front of the TV or the computer monitor, or having meaningless conversations with close friends about who is doing what, with whom. There is simply is no space for reading books, learning new skills, or organizing your closet. As you sober up, you will find that you have a vast amount of free time, which you can now use to your advantage.

An even more amazingly, you will find that you start to care about other people. In my case, as a self-centered drunk, I was happiest alone, with a bottle of wine or whiskey and an internet connection. Dealing with other people's problems was, quite frankly, not *my* problem. I was successful; they weren't. So they didn't interest me.

With the help of AA and my newfound sobriety, I realized relatively quickly that other people were, in fact, *very* interesting to me, regardless of their economic circumstances. I started conversing with down-and-out drunks, people from all walks of life, and the more I did so, the more I became aware that my story was far from unique. I learned that we are all in this together. I sincerely believe you will go through a similar transformation.

I would like to state right here that I owe a lot to the organization that is AA. It's really an amazing brotherhood of fellow human beings that even non-drunks would be lucky to have. The level of honesty and integrity you find in AA is just off the charts – nobody is ever that honest or that clear in their analysis of themselves in any other forum of human interaction. I wouldn't change much about AA, but I do have some "updates" that I would like to bring to the program. Think of them as suggestions for stopping drinking in the 21st century.

As I will discuss later, I don't agree with AA that it is necessary to ask the forgiveness of a "higher power of your own understanding". Before joining AA, I was an atheist, and I am still an atheist one year later. I think (and know) that you can absolutely kick alcohol without having to convert to some spiritual belief system. The key thing, however -- and this is probably why AA is so successful -- is that you need to make sure you don't think of yourself as that higher power.

One of the side effects of alcohol is that it focuses you entirely inwards, giving you the false impression that you are the center of the universe (in much the same way that in 1400, the Christian religion was convinced the sun and all the planets revolved around the Earth). Getting rid of that self-obsession, and realizing that you really aren't all that special is pretty key (in my opinion) to stopping drinking.

Another major area of focus in this book is fitness. The image of AA – dirty old men in raincoats drinking coffee and smoking in front of churches and community gathering places -- is, sadly, somewhat accurate. My feeling is that drinking gallons of coffee and replacing alcohol with nicotine is not the way to go. The "Krueger Method", if I can call it that, is to drop alcohol, as well as all other contaminants in your life, in one fell swoop.

If you stop drinking, keeping all else equal, you will lose a lot of weight and feel *much* better. That's not the case if you replace drinking with eating candy, desserts, or other unhealthy carbohydrates. And smoking is, unconditionally, an awful habit. It's right up next to alcohol as a horrible addiction. If you do smoke, I think you are going to have a hard time kicking the alcohol habit while still maintaining your pack-a-day nicotine routine.

The human body is a miraculously complex thing. It has evolved to survive for months without eating; is capable of walking for hundreds of miles on water alone; and has developed the capacity to think on its own, make tools, and live peacefully in tribes of other humans. If you take that same body, feed it processed foods, over-saturate it with fats and carbohydrates, leave it under-exercised, and expose it to a toxic and addictive chemical called ethanol, you should not be surprised when it quickly degenerates.

We are born to look like the classical Da Vinci "Vitruvian Man": lean, fit and perfectly proportioned. Through the "miracle" of modern life and technology, we are evolving into obese addicts with a bad case of Attention Deficit Disorder; we consume "pop culture" as if it were, in fact, a type of "culture"; and we isolate behind our computers and mobile phones. This, folks, is *not* the way it was meant to be. I can't convince billions of people to change, but I just might be able to convince *you*. And that's enough for me.

THE 1%

In the computer hacker group "Anonymous", much is made of the top "1%" who are busy ruining it for the rest of the 99%. But when you stop drinking completely, you begin to realize you make up a very small group of people on this planet who are completely sober.

I don't know if it is 1% or 5%, but it's a small number (at least in non-Arabic countries). Drinking is embedded into almost every major human activity: wine at meals, beer and liquor at bars, alcohol on airplanes, liquor stores on every street corner. When you meet a friend or a date, your first thought is, "Let's grab a drink".

Being in the 1% club has amazing benefits:

- You will definitely lose weight (I lost 35 pounds)

- Overall you will be in much better physical shape

- You will feel much more calm and grounded

- You will think much clearer (and faster)

- You will take a greater interest in other people

- You will feel more connected with the world in general

- You will appreciate music, movies and other entertainment far more

As I mentioned earlier, for an alcohol user, a life without drinking may seem flat and unbearable. But this again is your brain tricking you – it's the virus talking. In reality, the exact opposite is true: your life will be much more enjoyable without alcohol than with it.

It's a difficult transition, but one that I wholeheartedly recommend. And of course, you can always go back. If you try sobriety for 90 days and decide it's not for you, the old path is just a drink away.

The first and most important step is just deciding that you want to live a healthy, fit, clean, and happy life. From my perspective, it's hard to imagine why you *wouldn't* want that, but I understand the tricks that alcohol and obesity play on a person's mind. An alcoholic or an addict always thinks that life without drinking is hardly worth living; an overweight person always looks at exercise as a chore. In reality, you will be much happier living a clean and sober lifestyle, and you will look on exercise as a pleasure, exactly the same way you used to, as a child.

How you will react to a life without drugs or alcohol is your story to write. I am 100% sure, however, that you will thank me if this book in any way helps you to get there. You simply don't meet people who have quit and gone through the changes I describe who think fondly of starting up again. It's a new life, and it can be yours.

[2]

My Story

TO BEGIN, let me tell you a little bit about my story. I am in my early fifties, and have a PhD from Stanford University in the highly *non-related* field of operations research (roughly, "Applied Mathematics"). My qualifications for writing this book have absolutely nothing to with my degree or my knowledge of medicine (which is extremely rudimentary), but with the fact that I was successfully able to kick one of the most addictive substances known to man – alcohol.

As an aside, I will say that with the knowledge I now possess, I would completely distrust any book on alcohol or addiction written by a medical doctor. The medical profession has an absolutely horrible track record of dealing with alcohol addiction, or with wellness or fitness in general. Stopping drinking is not something for which you can get advice from your doctor. No pill known to man will cure you. The only possible way out is to listen to a former drunk, like me.

I would like to think of myself as a somewhat above average drunk, at least as far as mental capacity, but the truth is that my story is a textbook case of alcoholism, and could be told by any number of people. It just happens to be mine.

From my teenage years, all the way up to June 22, 2013 – the last day I had a drink – alcohol was an integral part of my life. Like everybody else, I drank in college. I drank in my twenties when I was a young trader on Wall Street. And I started seriously drinking in my thirties and forties as I became *very* successful financially.

My weapon of choice was red wine, ideally French, either from Bordeaux or Burgundy. I started collecting old bottles, learned the names of obscure chateaux, and formed an opinion on what were the great vintages and which ones were overrated. I dreamt of someday owning a vineyard, and drinking myself to death in my retirement somewhere along the French countryside (after trolling around Parisian bars and restaurants, like Hemingway). When friends stopped by, I pulled out one obscure bottle after another from my collection, and lectured them on what made that bottle special.

Not satisfied entirely with wine, I made a foray into the world of single-malt whiskey, and started cultivating a status as, "somebody who really knew his whiskies". I would tell people that Macallan 12 is really superior to Macallan 18 despite the lower price, but that a specific occasion really called for a "peaty" Langavulin.

While all this "alcohol education" was taking place, in many respects my life was falling apart. I started gaining weight, always slowly, but also always steadily. Once a skinny kid at Stanford, I hit close to 200 pounds by age 48. My eyes were baggy; my health had deteriorated to the point where I loathed any form of physical activity. I hated looking at myself in the mirror.

I went on several "detox holidays" and lost some weight, but the weight quickly came back, and the other symptoms – high blood pressure, falling asleep as early as 9pm, extremely low stamina, snoring, complete lack of interest in anything sexual – remained.

My physical condition was objectively quite poor. One friend after another would comment that, "I looked terrible," and that, "I should really try drinking less," but none of these words of caution had any effect.

And then things went from bad to worse. Increased stress at my job, combined with the painkillers offered by a friend, led to a quick, downward spiral.

Over a three-month span, I went from drinking a bottle of wine most nights, to drinking a bottle and a half every day, and supplementing that with 4 or 5 Vicodin pills. I had officially gone off the ledge. Drinking was now no longer reserved for nighttime. I would drink at lunch as well, and most of the early evening before I went home and started the "real" drinking.

I began to black out. Once a week or more, I would have a very hard time remembering exactly what had happened during these lapses of consciousness. I had a long drive home every night, and almost one night out of two, I would have to take a cab home because I was too drunk to drive. The other night I was probably also *legally* too drunk to drive, but I made the choice to "wing it" and rely on cruise control, an open window and my prayers to the gods not to get pulled over.

Amazingly, I defied the odds. I was stopped several times, but managed to keep a straight face and drive on through. Other nights, I would see the police up ahead and quickly pull over to the side of the road ahead of the roadblock. It was painful, but I never got caught.

At night, I would have to drink more and more just to fall asleep. I would keep bottles (of whiskey, typically) stashed in my closet for when I would wake up at one in the morning, needing just a bit more alcohol to quiet down. I would literally crawl in bed, sometimes with all my clothes on, and just pass out.

None of this *seemed* to interfere directly with my professional work. From 9am to 5pm, I managed to function cogently at work, with the caveat that mornings were always rough on account of the hangovers (and sometimes the period after lunch was a blur from the three-wine-glass lunch).

I should mention, since the reader will wonder, what I do. The best way I can describe it is, "I am in the internet sector". Generally speaking, that means that I start companies, raise money, invest my own money and sometimes sell the companies I start for a huge profit. I've been doing it for a long time, and have had a string of successful "exits", meaning big, multi-million dollar payouts. And all of this while drinking very steadily! No apparent problems on the professional side; on the contrary, it might seem that, like the Mad Men of TV, alcohol was an ingredient in my success.

My family life was a different matter. When I did get home, I was either completely drunk, or in a hurry to get drunk then and there. The idea of listening to my wife's day was, quite frankly, an interruption to the most important task at hand, i.e. opening a bottle of whatever was available and drinking it straight down.

On June 21, 2013, I received an email from my wife telling me she was filing for divorce. Two hours later, an agent showed up at my office and handed me my divorce papers. I had been served.

For the next 36 hours, I drank heavily, polishing off at least two pints of whiskey. The world was completely black, and the whiskey wasn't working fast enough. I was oscillating between sober and depressed, and completely drunk and depressed. There seemed to be absolutely no solution.

Then, the next day, I stumbled into an Alcoholics Anonymous meeting. It seemed like a complete long shot, and I wasn't taking it very seriously. Maybe I could clean myself up for a few weeks so I could get a better idea of what to do. In any case, I certainly wasn't planning on stopping drinking for any substantial amount of time.

As I sat down, I felt a certain energy in the room that I had never felt before. People seemed very eager to sit down and get the meeting started. The mood seemed happy, almost euphoric. This struck me as odd because, by any definition, these were society's biggest losers. What possible reason could they have for *celebrating* on a Sunday at ten-thirty in the morning?

Then, as in all AA meetings, newcomers were asked to self-identify. When my turn came around, it was easy enough to say, "Fred, Alcoholic". I was just following the pattern. Then, something strange happened. As I said my name and the word "alcoholic", a wave of realization came over me that, in fact, I had a really serious problem with alcohol and I wanted out.

In the next few minutes, random strangers started sharing their personal stories of recovery with a kind of honesty I had never heard before or since outside of an AA meeting. I suddenly raised my hand (even though that wasn't the protocol) and was called on to share.

Within an hour, I had shared the story of my divorce, my struggle with drinking, and my desire to stop with 50 complete strangers. It was cathartic, and I couldn't stop the tears. At the end of the meeting, other AA members gave me hugs and telephone numbers. "When's your next meeting?" they asked. "Call me anytime. Let's go to a meeting together".

That night, I wrote the following on Facebook:

> If you are reading this, you may, like myself, have a very false idea of what AA meetings are about. First of all, you might think that they are filled with "cultists", members who are trying to force their religious views on you. This is incorrect. While the idea of "total surrender" is completely key to AA, I don't take this necessarily to mean a belief in a Christian god. I, for one, have a hard time with that specific concept, as I have shared with many of you privately and publicly. That doesn't mean I don't believe that there is something that is bigger than all of us. In fact, it just might be that "all of us" are just cells of a global "organism" that evolves and exists independently of us.
>
> The point is, surrender means you acknowledge that addiction is a physical problem that can't simply be stopped by willpower. You need to realize that it is bigger than your willpower, and can only effectively be solved

by having the willingness to have the willingness to accept change. (Kind of meta, but accurate).

AA is also filled with very interesting, attractive people of both genders. Some of the men seemed just about the sharpest guys I have met in a long time. I think that the effect of being "as dry as a bone" clearly helps one's thought process.

But more than just sharp, the people there seem to be phenomenal listeners. Clearly the self-reflective nature of the process is just great all around. People are actually thinking about others and about themselves in a kind of honest way that I have not observed in the past.

So I will definitely continue. I may not make it. But I think it's a phenomenal idea, and for me, the best way to attack what I now realize is an addiction, plain and simple, that I will have for the rest of my life, sober or not."

I was not aware at the time that AA disparages talking about the program in public, and in particular, on Facebook. The origin of this secrecy dates back to the 1930's when AA was founded, when the words "rehab" and

"alcoholic" couldn't be mentioned in mixed company.
Today, in 2014, this tenet seems completely anachronistic.
Shouldn't AA or any other such organization have a serious
Internet presence?

[3]

A Type of Virus

ALL FORMS of ingestible alcohol boil down to a single molecule: ethanol. Ethanol consists of two carbon atoms, 6 hydrogen atoms and one oxygen atom.

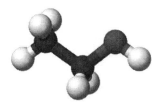

Figure 1 The ethanol molecule

Whether you are drinking a great French wine, a glass of whiskey, a pint of beer or a shot of tequila, that molecule is what is going to get you drunk.

If you don't remember your high school chemistry, the two black atoms forming the "base" of the ethanol molecule are carbon atoms. They also function as the building blocks for both coal and diamonds. The white atoms are hydrogen. The red atom is oxygen, a staple of the air we breathe and the water we drink. When hydrogen, carbon and oxygen are combined, they make up "carbohydrates", which are responsible for many components in the human body, including glycogen, DNA and RNA.

For what it is worth, the process of "getting drunk" works as follows: The ethanol molecule interacts with another oxygen atom to produce acetaldehyde, or "ethanal".

$$CH_3CH_2-OH \longrightarrow H_3C-C\overset{\displaystyle O}{\underset{\displaystyle O-H}{}}$$

The oxidation of ethanol

This oxidation process – the creation of the acetaldehyde – happens when too much ethanol enters the system before it can be metabolized by the liver.

The more acetaldehyde you have in your system, the more of a hangover you will have. Over time, your liver will metabolize the ethanol, and your hangover will disappear. It appears that various races have different reactions to acetaldehyde. Asians, for example, react to it very badly. This might explain why there are fewer drunks in Asia on a per capita basis than say, North America or Europe.

Now while the ethanol molecule is at the heart of all alcoholism, there are other molecules for other drugs, including prescription drugs, that have many of same side effects as alcohol, i.e., addiction, a false feeling of well-being, isolation etc. The point is not that addiction is a problem with ethanol per se, but that the culprit, has, for every single drug, been completely identified. And they all work in the same way: like a virus.

To be clear:

When you ingest alcohol (or drugs), it is as if you are introducing a computer virus into your brain.

How the virus works

The first thing the virus does is to silence and relax any part of the brain that was busy worrying. This is purely a chemical reaction. As the ethanol molecules penetrate your neural network, the precise electrical connections needed to create these worries misfire.

As your concerns dissipate, you start to feel a hazy sense of well-being. It's as if your brain were in a cloud, and although you realize that you are not thinking normally, the centers of worry disappear one after the other.

The brain's controller mechanism mistakenly identifies this state as a good thing. It triggers other signals to go get more of whatever caused the happy cloud.

Ethanol chain reaction

→ Electrical connections in brain impaired

→ Worries disappear

→ Controller identifies this as a positive event

→ Triggers desire for more alcohol

Once this cycle has been established, the identification in the brain of "alcohol = good" can persist for a very long time, potentially for the entire life of your brain (i.e., your life). It can also be – and usually is -- a dormant, subconscious identification that can be triggered by any number of events or emotions.

All humans will react to this feedback loop in the same way, but it is stronger in some than in others. For some people, the controller mechanism identifies the worry-free state as not only good, but "fantastic", saying, "Give me as much of this substance as I can possibly get". This desire for oblivion is the mark of a true alcoholic.

It seems that repeated use reinforces the feedback loop. The identification "alcohol = good" is engraved more deeply into the brain's memory with every experience. Notably, this buildup may be entirely subconscious. After 10 years of drinking, you might suddenly find yourself not just wanting to drink, but *needing* to drink, as the neural connections that form these desires have become firmly entrenched.

Conversely, non-use dulls the association. After not drinking for about 3 months, the urgent pangs to have a drink disappear. There are, however, remaining dormant desires, which might be – and usually are -- enough to trigger the need for a first drink. Once the familiar pattern emerges, the brain's pattern-matching mechanism then strongly recalls the stored, dormant connections, triggering an uncontrollable urge to have the second drink.

The key thing to realize is that the brain is being tricked into believing something is good for it, which in fact isn't. While alcohol appears to be "solving" problems, it is really just dulling the problem-perception centers. For instance, if you have financial problems before drinking, you still have them after drinking. The fact that the brain was "worrying" about these problems in the first place is a symptom of the brain trying to solve these issues – a positive and necessary thing.

Fighting a virus once you have been infected is extremely difficult, precisely because "you" are no longer in charge. Every thought you have, every move you instinctively make, every brilliant "solution" to your problems needs to be reexamined to see whether it is truly in your best interest. Much of what will go on in your head, especially when you initially stop drinking, will be the virus looking for more alcohol.

OTHER PEOPLE'S STORIES

One of the most amazing things about AA is that you listen to hundreds of people tell you what it was like when they were drinking or using. A few stories stand out in my mind, which I am happy to share with the reader. I've changed a few names and places to protect the privacy of all involved, but the stories are all very real.

CHRISTINE

The first is the story of Christine, a middle-aged woman who grew up in Pacific Palisades. Christine was a cheerleader in high school, and became the perfect suburban mom before alcohol (and then drugs) brought her down. Looking at her today, you might think you are talking to the school librarian; it's almost inconceivable to think that ten years ago she was a meth addict, lived in a crack house, and was known as a "tweaker" (somebody who would go for two weeks at a time without sleep).

Christine spent time in a woman's prison before an old high school friend bailed her out and checked her into a recovery center. With less than $20 to her name, she left the rehab for a motel in the worst part of LA, daughter in tow, only to witness a mid-afternoon shooting and have the victim bleed to death in her arms. That, apparently, was enough to set her on the right path for good. Today, Christine makes working with other recovering alcoholics her main priority.

FRANK

The second story is about my friend Frank, who managed a family-owned restaurant in New York City in his early twenties, while at the same time enjoying an industrial strength Xanax and cocaine habit. I didn't realize you could actually buy Xanax in 5,000-pill bags, but you can, and Frank did. Like many others, he sold drugs to finance his own drug habit, but even then, he came up short and had to steal to make ends meet.

After spending a weekend holed up in a Chelsea hotel with two prostitutes, several ounces of coke, hundreds of Xanax pills, and copious bottles of vodka, he got a call from his family inquiring why several hundred thousand dollars were missing from the family business. Rather than confess his crime and admit his habit, he did what others have done before him – he took a greyhound bus to the west coast, and started from scratch with no phone, no credit card, no place to live.

JUSTIN

The third story is about a writer I met whom I will call Justin. Like many writers, Justin enjoyed a scotch or two while racking his brains to create the next great American novel. He was clever enough to realize that his 10-scotch-a-night habit was getting in the way of his productivity, however, and came up with an innovative solution: He would start drinking at midnight, and would only keep enough scotch on hand to last until two in the morning, when the LA bars close.

His plan was going great until just after 2 a.m., when he finished his third double scotch. Unfortunately, he then realized he absolutely needed to have more. With all the bars and liquor stores closed, he only had one alternative. He would have to call a friend and get alcohol from him. Being that he was relatively new to LA at the time and didn't know very many people in the area, this was not an easy task. He did, however, know an old friend in San Diego, and reasoned that the traffic would be light in the middle of the night.

For those not familiar with California geography, San Diego is a good three hours' drive from LA, even when there is no traffic. But this did not stop our friend, who I am sure was legally drunk at the time. In any case, shortly after 5 a.m., Justin arrived in

San Diego and began drinking beers with his buddy. By 6 a.m., they both had the "eureka" moment that the beach bars would now be open; they proceeded to hit them in earnest.

Sometime later in the afternoon, Justin awoke on a raft, floating around in some swimming pool that he didn't recognize. The entire left side of his body had been baking in the sun. He now looked like some batman villain: one side burnt bright red, the other pale white. Slowly, he got off the raft and took stock of his surroundings. He heard a baby crying, and found it sitting in a crib nearby. He had no idea whose house it was or how he got there.

Eventually, he made his way back to LA that night and recounted the story to one of his drinking buddies. "Does this mean I am an alcoholic?" he questioned. "Absolutely not," replied the friend. "A true alcoholic would go back again tonight." Which, of course, Justin did.

BOB

Another favorite story of mine is the story of Bob, an alcoholic from Dallas, Texas, where, in his own words, "They give you a six-pack of beer and a rifle at birth."

Bob led a straightforward, alcoholic life. He drank heavily and owned a bar (to gain better access to his supply). But it was when he was introduced to the cruise industry that the fun and games really started.

Bob became the entertainment director for one of the largest cruise lines on the planet. "I loved buying people drinks," he explained. "But now, I was being paid to do it." He was so good at his new job that he rarely made it out of bed before noon on account of his typical hangover. And then, the drinking generally started all over again.

One particular day, while ashore in some Caribbean country, he suddenly realized that the final cruise gala was starting in just a few minutes. He, of course, was the Master of Ceremonies. Over ten thousand people were anxiously waiting for him to deliver the opening remarks on a four-story stage bigger than the Dolby Theatre in Hollywood. He stumbled back to the boat, grabbed a suit and headed down the aisle towards the main stage. To his surprise, he was stopped by a security guard.

"You don't understand," he said. "I am the MC." "No," said the security guard, "You don't understand. I need you to pee in a cup. Now."

A few minutes later, our protagonist was in one of the men's rooms on the deck of the second largest ocean liner in the world, getting tested for drugs. But the person before him had not flushed! Ingeniously, Bob grabbed the cup and filled it directly from the toilet. The security guard took out a testing strip and shook his head. Somehow Bob had passed the test!

This story gets even better, however. Shortly after the incident, Bob was told by the cruise line that he had two choices: either quit now, or get fired in a few weeks when he was caught again. He chose to quit and move to California. One week later, he got his first DUI. A month after that, he got his second.

In the country jail, while awaiting his fate, he met a down-and-out looking individual. The dialog went something like this:

Bob: "What are you in here for?"

Down-and-out man: "Murder. You?"

Bob: "Second DUI."

Down-and-out man: "Wow. That's bad news."

Bob then realized that if a murderer was telling him it was bad news, it *really was bad news*. And sure enough, he was sent to a prison in Downtown LA -- a very different place than country jail.

On arrival, he showed the guards a bit of lip. Didn't these dudes realize he was one the good guys? He was an ex-entertainment director of a cruise ship, after all. Unfortunately, his efforts at talking his way out of the situation seemed to have no effect. Or did they? When everybody else was handed the traditional prison striped outfit, he was handed a green gown. "What, am I special?" he asked. "Oh yeah," came the response. "You are special, all right. You're going *upstairs*, buddy".

As it turns out, upstairs was the mental ward. And, yes, apparently it was exactly like "One Flew Over The Cuckoo's Nest", right down to his first lasting image of the place: an inmate banging his head against a glass window until he started bleeding...

ALICE

A similar story in many respects belongs to Alice, a music industry executive who lived for years in New York, before moving back to Hollywood. The reason for her departure? She wanted to get back to "solid values" (which were conceivably at odds with the "crazy values" of Manhattan).

After some very light drinking with a good friend of hers (several bottles of wine each), Alice decided that she was in perfect shape to drive home. Somewhere along the way, she didn't see the other car coming, hit it, and spun around. Alice was fine, but she was so drunk that she literally fell asleep at the wheel, only to wake up in handcuffs while being escorted to jail.

Like Bob, she tried to convince the jail officer that there was some kind of mistake, and that she was a "good person" (unlike the other bad people in the jail facility). Could she please be let out? And by the way, how was the other person doing that she hit?

Sadly, that other person died shortly afterwards. Alice ended up spending six months in jail, which she came to feel "were not as bad as living her life as a drunk". Amazingly, great things can come out of every experience. In her case, that tragedy marked the beginning of her sobriety. She hasn't had a drink since.

VERONICA

If you think you had it rough as a teenager, you should meet Veronica. At just 21, she was a three-time heart transplant patient.

I met Veronica at the Marina Center, at the late night 11 p.m. AA meeting, which is something similar to the Michael Jackson "Thriller" video, with zombies popping up left and rightIn . In AA, there is a reverse correlation between the time of day of the meeting and the age of the participants. At 11pm, most of the drunks were under 25, and all of them were severely down and out.

Veronica stood out among those sorry souls with a tale that was fit for the "Twilight Zone". A chronic cocaine abuser from age 12, she literally burned out one heart after another with massive drug use. She was now hobbling along on heart number 4. How her parents continued to fund these heart transplants and not do something about her addiction was astounding. I am still baffled that she was even alive to tell her story.

These stories are just a few in the thousands of stories the average AA visitor will hear in the first 9 months. There are commonalities – the mental obsession with alcohol, the inability when drinking to see the consequences, and the effect of alcohol on both yourself and others.

[4]

How to Stop Drinking

ONCE YOU HAVE been drinking regularly for many years, it is extremely difficult to stop. Your brain becomes strongly wired to want alcohol. Any number of events or emotions can trigger the desire for a first drink, and once that *first drink* is in your system, the desire for a *second drink* can be uncontrollable.

As someone who has completely stopped drinking, I can tell you what works to get sober.

I've broken it down to 5 Rules. Not 12 steps as in AA, but 5 basic, common sense principles that you should make a point to follow – especially during the first 90 days. None of them involve God or a "higher power", and none of them involve going around to everybody you have wronged (like the lead character in the TV Show "My Name is Earl") asking for forgiveness.

We'll go over each one in detail, but here they are for reference:

RULE 1: Talk To Other Sober People

RULE 2: Realize What You Are Up Against

RULE 3: Make A Complete Transformation

RULE 4: Accept That You Are Not The Center of the Universe

RULE 5: Keep A Diary

I think it's very important to distinguish what it takes to *get* sober from what it takes to *stay* sober. Honestly, with only a short period of sobriety under my belt, I am not in a position to lecture on the latter. I will say, however, just from what I hear at AA meetings, that the single biggest obstacle to staying sober is attempting to go at it solo – not attending meetings, and not talking to other sober people.

But that's a different battle, and perhaps a different book that I should write ten years from now if I am still around to write it. At the moment, I want to focus on the already quite challenging task of *getting sober*.

It really is all about the first 90 days. Once you clean yourself out – from the inside – and start the intense physical transformation that accompanies stopping drinking, you will be on the right path. And from there, life gets a lot less difficult and a lot more enjoyable than you can imagine.

So let's dive into the 5 things you need to focus on in the initial phase of your recovery:

RULE 1: TALK TO OTHER SOBER PEOPLE

First of all, it's highly desirable to talk with other people who have stopped drinking, and to do so repeatedly. Alcoholics Anonymous functions as a central meeting point for the small minority of us who are completely sober. Just listening to other people's stories on how *they* kicked the habit seems to be the best defense against starting again. After 100 or so AA meetings, I generally don't learn something at every meeting, but I always do feel better when I am done.

If you are just starting with sobriety, you are bound to get a ton of bad advice from your friends or romantic partners who are on the other side. "One drink can't kill you"; "A glass of wine a day is healthy"; "Wine with meals is fine"; "Let's just celebrate this once" and so on...

In the same way, talking with people who have actually kicked the addiction will give you the faith that you too can kick it. Listening to other former drunks talk about what it was like when they drank or used will make you smile as you realize that we all are much more similar than we thought. Every drunk hides alcohol, every drunk lies to himself or herself, every drunk imagines complex schemes for slowing down or controlling drinking – schemes that inevitably fail.

As one person that I met in AA said in her "share", AA is "the best show in town." And this is Los Angeles, the entertainment capital of the world. From a pure entertainment point of view, you can't beat the variety and comic relief of some the stories you will hear in the rooms of AA.

To get a sense of these stories, just pick up a copy of the AA *Big Book*. While written in 1939, the stories of alcoholics trying to quit in the second half of the book ring as true today as they did 70 years ago.

It's tempting to fill up a hundred pages or so right here with some of the crazy testimonials that I have heard in AA, and keep hearing at every meeting I go to. One common thread is that massive, transformational change is absolutely possible. I've met ex-gang members who now are AA treasurers, ex-crack addicts who look like personal trainers, ex-homeless people with wives, kids and jobs.

However bad you think you have it, think again. Some of the people you will meet in AA have all of the same problems you have – times 10. Do you have a roof over your head? A car? An actual job? Haven't killed anybody yet? Consider yourself lucky. You will meet a lot of people in AA who started where you are today, and went a lot further south before they hit bottom.

By the way, it's perfectly fine to go to meetings and say absolutely nothing. 90% of the benefit of the meeting comes from just listening, and if anything, more people want to talk than there is time. Considering there are meetings everywhere – in every possible part of the world every single day – there are very few excuses not to go. Just go to a meeting finder online, find a free hour in your schedule, and hop in your car for a quick drive. You will be immersed in recovery talk in no time at all.

Rule 2: Make Sure You Know What You Are Up Against

Stopping drinking is not an easy thing. One of the biggest mistakes people make is underestimating the power of the opponent. As mentioned in Chapter 3, you might as well have the view that your entire brain has been taken over by a type of virus – because that's very close to the truth.

What that means is that after you take that first drink, you will not be able to control your second. As they say in AA, "You buy the first drink, the first drink buys the second, and the second drink buys you". You simply can't be "a bit sober" after a life of drinking; you need to either be 100% or not at all.

There will be a lot of opportunities to have that first drink – some of them seemingly harmless. New Year's Eve, for instance. How bad could it be to have a glass of champagne? Or perhaps you are on an 8-hour flight. Wouldn't you like a glass of wine with your meal? Why not?

I can tell you from hanging out at AA meetings that when people relapse, they relapse quickly. Even after years of not drinking, just a single drink is enough to send most ex-drinkers back to past habits in a flash. How quickly? *Within days,* usually. The memory cells that recorded "alcohol = good" are still in your brain, just waiting to get reactivated.

One of the reasons AA gives out chips at various stages of sobriety is to celebrate intermediate victories. One day sober? Phenomenal. One month? Amazing. Ninety days? Come to the front of the room and get a hug. Nobody in AA will judge you because you have "only" 43 days. Everybody who has kicked the habit remembers how hard it was in the beginning. And we all want you to succeed.

One of the very hard realities of stopping drinking is coming to grips with the fact that there are no middle-ground solutions. As much as I would have loved to find a way to continue drinking just a glass or so of fine French wine every night, I know now that in my case that is just not possible. It is my best guess that in your case as well there is no "moderate path".

Almost anything can cause a relapse. One fellow I met in AA who had 3 years sober recounted meeting a gorgeous exchange student from Sweden once on the street in Venice, CA. The girl asked him, innocently enough, if he knew of any good bars nearby. One hour later, he found himself with the exchange student, ten shots in, at a dive bar on the beach. It took him another 2 years to get sober again.

Even people with considerable amounts of time can succumb. It doesn't mean that sobriety is hopeless; it just means you must always stay on your guard. And don't be fooled for a minute that painkillers or pot are "OK". There is no surer way to fall off the wagon than to take a few painkillers, or to enjoy a simple joint amongst friends. It's not about the type of chemical; it's the process of self-obliteration. All roads lead to the same oblivion.

As I mention later in the book, you will need to be especially wary of bad influences: toxic people, places, and environments. Everywhere you look, you will invariably find someone pushing alcohol. Parties, events, celebrations, business functions, even religious ceremonies will all be filled with landmines you will have to carefully avoid. You can certainly try to date a drinker, for example, but I seriously doubt that will work for you, especially in the early stages of your sobriety. There is nothing to *prevent* you from hanging out at bars and night clubs, but that would not be a smart move -- unless you want to quickly go back to where you came from.

RULE 3: MAKE A COMPLETE TRANSFORMATION

The third major principal you should embrace is not just stopping alcohol, but any other bad habits as well – in particular, bad food choices and smoking. Stopping drinking will help you on a major path to physical recovery, but the single best way to really stay sober is to fundamentally change your *entire body.*

This is not as crazy as it might sound. Let's take a heavy drinker (like I used to be), who ingests a bit more than 2,000 calories a day and gets 800 or so calories from alcohol. To put this in perspective, the average bottle of wine contains 650 calories, and a six-pack of beer has 900 calories. If you can cut out the drinking without doing anything else, you will lose a pound of fat every 4 days! (A pound of fat equals about 3,500 calories).

On the other hand, it's pretty easy to replace the alcohol with other "feel good" calories. Since alcohol is metabolized very similarly to the way sugar is metabolized, people who quit alcohol usually get a craving for sugar. Three donuts are equivalent to a bottle of wine – and if you are not careful, you will eat all the calories you avoided by not drinking.

In order to not replace drinking with compulsive eating, I strongly suggest monitoring everything that goes in your system on the day you stop drinking. There are many great tools for this. I recommend the site Lose It (loseit.com) and the fitness band/service FitBit (fitbit.com). Both of these offer excellent ways for you to enter everything you eat into a database. They also allow you to track your physical activity.

With respect to exercise, you should exercise for an hour at least twice a week. If you don't, you are simply cheating your body. Any kind of exercise is good. Walking in particular is great; it can be done anywhere. I suggest going above and beyond the minimum, however, and actually getting some form of exercise every day, even if only for 30 minutes.

Much has been made of the technology of various bands and clip-on devices such as FitBit and Fuel Band. These are all very cool gadgets, but the reality is that weight loss is primarily (80%) about eating correctly, not how much you exercise. In particular, I actually question whether sporadic exercise is even a good thing. Very often, people overeat following a big workout. Exercise is more about consistency than quantity.

With a reasonable diet and moderate exercise, you should be able to lose between a pound and a pound and a half per week. It's very important that you measure your weight as much as possible –daily, if you can – but don't focus so much on any individual day's weight; focus on the lowest point you have achieved so far.

I personally use a spreadsheet (Google Docs) to keep track of my lowest weight. If I had tracked the actual weight, the variations would be all over the place, as any individual reading depends completely on how much water you have in your system. But if you focus on the low readings, you should see a steady drop. The weight loss will taper off at times as your lifestyle changes (long trips, for example, tend to be bad for weight loss), but you will lose weight just like clockwork.

One of the real advantages of combining a fitness regime with stopping drinking is that you have some absolute, measurable indicators (your weight and body mass) to indicate your progress on the road to recovery. While weight loss is not by any means the only objective here, having measurable targets help. I see so many people in AA who just drift from meeting to meeting, without any clear sense of how far they have come, or where they are going. You don't have to follow their example.

RULE 4: ABANDON THE IDEA THAT YOU ARE NOT THE CENTER OF THE UNIVERSE

The third thing is to abandon the belief that you are self-important. This is my rewrite of the AA "step" that asks you to place your trust in a "higher power of your understanding". Let's be clear: most of us no longer believe in a God in the sense that nearly everybody did 200 years ago. There is now a very believable scientific explanation for how we got here, for how the universe was formed, etc. God, or even some convoluted "energy" is just not *needed* as an explanation. But on the other hand, the alcoholic mind is relentlessly self-centered and believes that it is completely in control, immortal, invulnerable and infallible. That belief has to be eradicated if you want to get sober.

To expand on this a bit, repeated alcohol use knocks out your worries and inhibitions one after the other and makes you feel like the only thing in the universe – powerful, all knowing, and detached from your body. In other words, it makes you feel like (a) god. To kick this habit, you need to convince yourself that in fact you aren't a god, that you do live in a fragile body, and that your thought processes have been corrupted by a long term, insidious virus called ethanol.

Anything helps. Looking at the immensity of the ocean and realizing the smallness of your role on the planet (and beyond) helps. Going to a church or meditation group helps. Anything that will help you escape the flawed belief system that you are self-important and in control is good.

Rule 5: Keep a Diary

Most successful technology startups operate using the concept of "Key Performance Indicators" –

or KPIs for short. This could be, for example, the total number of visitors to your website, your gross profit margin, or the number of happy employees. These are simply metrics by which you judge progress. Amazingly, if you set goals for yourself and you actually *measure* your progress towards achieving these goals, you will do better than somebody who just "drifts along".

The personal and physical transformation I am talking about here is tough. Your best shot at achieving it is to keep a private, personal diary of how you are doing on a daily basis. As you work your way through sobriety -- and weight loss – your progress will be there on the page for you to see.

I recommend two ways of keeping a diary. The first is simply to start a Microsoft Word document and just add entries to it every day. You can use a service like Dropbox to keep the document backed up on the web, because you will definitely not want to lose it.

The second way is to use the free posting and blogging service "Mozart" that I created. You can set up an account at www.Mozart.co. Mozart will allow you to create a set of private posts that you can access from your desktop, iPad or smartphone (iPhone or Android). It has portability advantages over the Word file and is shareable. This is a great thing if, like me, you end up wanting to share your story with others.

Each diary entry should contain a summary of how you feel that day, and what you have learned. If you do go to AA (which I recommend) you will meet a lot of people very quickly. The diary will be useful in keeping names and stories straight.

DIFFERENCES WITH AA

So, how do my five rules compare to the 12 "steps" of AA? Well, to begin with, they are not meant to be consecutive; they're just 4 things you need to keep your eye on at all times.

The first major difference is the inclusion of Rule 1, which surprisingly isn't in AA, although it is said repeatedly at AA gatherings. "Go to meetings"; "Show up"; "Be Present" – these are usually the first words spoken by every long-term member of AA. They've just never been officially added to the 12 steps.

The second difference is the explicit inclusion of Rule 2: Be aware of what you are up against. This again is talked about repeatedly in the AA *Big Book* and at AA meetings, but it really deserves to be highlighted. It doesn't take much to relapse; all you need is a single drink. In Chapter 3, I gave some pretty good reasons for why this cycle of addiction is so strong and why a casual quitter has really no chance against the "cunning and baffling beast" (AA's words) that is alcohol.

The next difference is the focus I place on a complete physical commitment. I am shocked that AA sanctions cigarette smoking outside of the meetings, and provides unlimited coffee, with sugar, and often cakes or other unhealthy foods at meetings. If the *Big Book* had been written today, I am certain that it would have included some focus on fitness. As it is, most AA literature was written in 1939, when absolutely nobody had any conception of personal fitness or wellness. I strongly believe that a physical transformation is your best defense against relapsing. If you can achieve what I achieved in just 6 months, you will never want to drink again.

The final major area of disagreement I have with AA is their thinly veiled edict that you need to turn your fate over to God. Just to be safe, the founders of AA chose the words, "A higher power of your own understanding", but in my experience, it's still an unnecessary component of recovery from addiction. In fact, in many cases, I think it actually hurts, as believing that you are inhabited by some kind of divine spirit can really cause you to lose track of your own body, and not get to my Step 3, which is your physical transformation.

I believe the fitness aspect of recovery is important enough to deserve its own chapter (see Chapter 6: A Complete Physical Transformation). I also think the religious angle deserves a lot more discussion, because this the number one problem people have with AA, and I think it's a very valid and real problem. I discuss this at length in Chapter 7.

A GENETIC THEORY

For the record, I would like to state a theory of mine on why so many of us have a predisposition towards alcoholism (beyond the "virus explanation" in Chapter 3).

That theory revolves around genetics. Because alcohol decreases sexual barriers in women, and increases confidence in men, alcoholics have a stronger bias than non-alcoholics towards passing on the alcohol-appreciation gene.

It's hard to quantify this theory, but it's clear that alcohol has been consumed by mankind for at least 5,000 years. That's some 250 generations. Running some quick numbers on the mathematics of population genetics shows that alcohol propensity could have easily tripled during this period. Over the next 5,000 years it is bound to only increase.

This solves the AA paradox that alcohol is apparently so damaging, but yet so widespread. Yes, it is bad for us humans, but it is great for the survival and replication of our pro-alcohol genes.

Please note: My address is listed on the front cover for the Nobel Prize in Medicine, or any award given by the New England Journal of Medicine.

[5]

A Complete Transformation

I WAS TALKING to a venture capitalist friend of mine the other day. He mentioned to me that if it were up to him, he would be funding "real problems", as opposed to fly-by-night social networks, video sites and ecommerce "shop of the month clubs". I asked him what he meant, and he responded, "I'm interested in hard science: quantum computers, better energy storage, electric cars and so on". I immediately replied that while these inventions might make the world a little better, the biggest problem we all face is simple: *we're overweight.*

Let's try to quantify exactly what that means, and how much of a problem it is.

According to an interesting government report I dug up on the internet, the average person in the United States has gained 24 pounds from 1960 to 2002. In other words, we are all, on average, gaining *half a pound of weight every year.*

For men 20 years or older, we're now up to a staggering 195 pounds each. Given that the average height for the same group is 5' 10", that's a full 35 pounds more than the recommended ideal weight of 160.

And that's just the average. For the same group, the Center of Disease Control defines being overweight as anything over 180 pounds. According to that metric, a staggering 74% of us are now officially in the red zone. For the same group, the word "obese" is meant to apply to people 210 pounds or higher. Over one person in three now falls into *that* category.

And this is not just an American phenomenon. Our bad diet and lifestyle is our number one export. The rest of the world is not far behind.

Being fat is no joke. You are far more susceptible to heart attacks or stoke; you feel awful, both physically and psychologically. You may have begun life as a healthy, skinny kid, but slowly turned into an immobile sack of fat that is awkward and unappealing.

The Physics of Weight Loss

Weight loss is a physical phenomenon, and one that is quite poorly understood by the average person.

To begin with, consider the following:

The only way you lose weight is by breathing.

As crazy as this may sound, this is, in fact, correct. Your body is an engine, which takes in food through your mouth, digests that food in your stomach and excretes it out as fecal matter. What goes in also goes out. With one big exception: your breathing.

As you inhale every 5 seconds or so, you fill your lungs with air, which is a mix of 78% nitrogen and 21% oxygen. The nitrogen doesn't interact much with your body, but the oxygen does, binding with carbon molecules (remember, our bodies are composed of long carbon and hydrogen chains). Exhaling then releases CO_2, or carbon dioxide, into the atmosphere.

It seems counter-intuitive that breathing could actually cause weight loss, but the numbers add up. The average breath is about half a liter, and 4.6% of that is CO_2. The density of CO_2 is 1.8kg per cubic meter, so (doing all the math), the average breath contains about 0.04 grams of CO_2– two fiftieths of a gram of CO_2.

Do that 20 times a minute, 60 minutes an hour, 24 hours a day and that's 14,000 breaths of air per day, 100,000 breaths a week. Those 100,000 breaths equal 2,000 grams or about 4 pounds, which is what you would lose in a week if you ate nothing.

By exercising you breathe more, and therefore burn more calories. But remember, fat is an extremely efficient form of energy storage; it takes an enormous amount of working out just to combat a single cheeseburger, or a single tablespoon of mayonnaise.

It also needs to be pointed out that fat people require exactly the same number of calories as thin people to maintain a constant weight. This seems counter-intuitive. How come the skinny person next to me can eat the same food as me and still stay skinny? The answer is that you get fat *slowly* – over time. Just an extra 300 calories a week difference between two people (one cheeseburger) will translate into an extra 4 pounds per year. After 10 years, one person remains thin while the other is 40 pounds overweight.

What this means is that in order to lose weight, you are going to have to make some adjustments to your overall calorie intake. I recommend a 25% drop in calories until you reach your desired weight. Depending on how fat you are, this could take anywhere from 3 months to a year. But don't despair; even if you are 70 pounds overweight, think of how good you will feel if you are *only* 35 pounds overweight. This is about incremental victories, not perfection.

Stopping Drinking as The First Step to Getting Fit

If you have not done so, you should consult a chart for what your ideal weight and body fat percentages should be. For example, a middle-aged 5' 10" male should weigh about 160 pounds. Not 185 pounds, which I estimated to be my "normal weight", or my peak weight of 200 pounds. If you are a 25-year-old woman at an average height of 5' 5", you need to start thinking 125 pounds – not 140 pounds or higher.

Sure, there are other things that matter physically. It's not all about weight. But the fact is, if you are 30 pounds overweight, you already have big problems. If you are 50 pounds or more overweight, you have absolutely no idea of what life could be like in the fitness zone.

Consider just the psychological impact. Even if you are happily married, do you want to be slim and attractive and appeal to your spouse? If you are dating, don't you think your chances of finding a great mate are much better in the fit zone? Do you really think a person who is fit would want to be with an overweight person like you?

I speak from experience. A few weeks after I stopped drinking, I noticed that my weight had dropped suddenly, all by itself. I wasn't doing anything different; I was simply abstaining from alcohol. As I mentioned in Chapter 3, the average drinker consumes at least 600 calories per day in pure ethanol. Cutting those calories out will almost guarantee that you lose a pound a week.

Now, most physical trainers will tell you NOT to measure your weight daily, as over any individual day, your weight can vary by as much as 4 or 5 pounds, depending on how much water is in your system. If you drink a lot of coffee, travel on a long airplane trip, or are otherwise stressed out, you will retain water. That's not a bad thing, but it means that you can't judge your progress based on any individual day's reading. However, you can still figure out how well you are doing if you look at your lowest weight over the last x days. In my case, I looked at my weight low over the last 7 days. Even though on several of those days my weight spiked high, the lows kept descending at a very constant rate.

I kept a simple spreadsheet of my weight, and recorded the low over the last 7 days. I used Google docs (they have a free online spreadsheet), but you can use Excel or even just a pad of paper or a book. I highly recommend an online system however, as pieces of paper are easily lost.

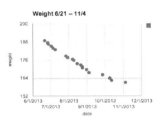

Figure 2 My initial weight loss.

So, how far do you have to go? Many people believe (falsely) that they will plateau at some percentage, even if they follow the plan to the letter. I have news for them: you will not plateau. If you eat less than 1,000 calories a day, you will not stop losing weight and you will eventually die. It's that simple.

Take a good look at yourself in the mirror and decide if you like the result. If your instinct is to look away, chances are you really need to lose weight. Simple as that.

As I mentioned in Chapter 3, I believe that getting your weight down in tandem with stopping drinking is your single best shot at staying sober. Think about it. Suppose you could transform yourself into a person 30 pounds lighter, placing you right in the "green zone" of every fitness chart. Suppose this body came with new energy, a better, more positive, attitude towards life, and better looks. Suppose that the new you kept getting complement after complement, with everybody asking, "What is your secret?" Don't you think then that you would seriously reconsider having even a single drink and risk going back to the old you?

In many ways, food addiction parallels alcohol and drug addiction. All of them play tricks on your brain to help you cope with your condition. Overweight people buy stretch pants, and wear sweatshirts and track suits to hide their obesity. They tend to move to suburbs with other overweight people, where their condition is not only tolerated, it's encouraged (exactly in the same way alcoholics tend to stick together and go drinking together).

FITNESS, NOT HEALTHCARE

If losing weight is so good for you, how come modern medicine is so clueless about it? How often has your doctor really, seriously got you to start on, and stay on a weight loss program?

The answer, unfortunately, is usually *"never"*. Doctors have evolved into prescription givers, in love with one pharmaceutical solution after the other. High cholesterol? Try Lipitor -- even though it has a long list of side effects. High blood pressure? There are many pills for that. Maybe you need a combination of prescriptions. In the modern day shortened doctor's visit, where the patient waits over a half hour in line to see a doctor for 10 minutes and is quickly sent packing with a list of pills to buy from the local pharmacy, there is really no time to monitor your overall well being or suggest long term changes.

Generally, losing weight is seen as the *patient's responsibility*, and coming up with a long list of prescribed pills is the *doctor's*. The kind of psychological training I am talking about here, such as asking the patient to write down everything he or she ate or drank, as well as their exercise levels, is rarely even considered.

The alternative medicine community is even worse – if you can believe that. Experts in "Chinese herbs", "acupuncture" and "energy work" are also fans of long prescription lists, but in their case the prescriptions don't actually do anything. How do I know? Because if they did, they would be called "medicine", not "alternative medicine". There is a lot of money to be made in solving actual medical problems.

If something like St. John's Wort was a solution, it would be recommended by the FDA. Granted, St. John's Wort is not patentable, but it still would be used to create some form of money-making, patentable drug. "Super St. John's Wort" from ELI Lilly unfortunately does not exist and never will. Because St. John's Wort does absolutely nothing, good or bad.

The solution to all of this is a focus on wellness as opposed to fixing health problems. Places like the Canyon Ranch in Arizona and Lanserhof in Austria are two very expensive but good programs that I have been to repeatedly. Unfortunately, wellness is not something to which you can apply shock therapy. You need to incorporate the teachings of these programs directly into your life. If you do, you won't need expensive detox centers.

If you do have the money, I suggest going to one of these "detox centers" around the time you stop drinking. It's money well spent. You will need to devote at least 2 weeks to your stay if you want to see any measurable results. But I can almost guarantee you will see results.

A NEW BUSINESS IDEA

In an ideal world, there would be something similar to a Starbucks on every corner devoted to monitoring your wellness. It would be a combination of measurements: weight, body fat, endurance tests, blood samples, and counseling. A wellness trainer would give you an assessment of how you are doing, would write notes in your electronic file, and would give you recommendations for the next week or weeks. This system would be very affordable – or even free – and be supported by the federal or state government.

If I wasn't busy with other projects, I might consider starting a chain of these fitness centers. The world certainly needs them. If you have the time and/or the money to go after it, feel free to steal the idea.

A FAT TAX

Fat people are a huge burden on society. As we grow into an increasingly overweight nation, even the slimmest amongst us are paying for the health problems of the majority of overweight and obese people. While it is doubtful that a mandated fat tax (weigh in every year and pay $x per pound overweight) would be politically achievable, we need to do everything possible to discourage people from choosing to overeat and reward those who don't.

If the average American adult man weighed 160 pounds as opposed to 200 pounds, our "healthcare problem" would simply go away. This is not a democratic vs. republican issue; both sides of the aisle are lobbied by aging, overweight seniors, by drug companies looking to push "solutions" instead of fix problems, and by the alcohol, fast food and hospitality industries, all of whom have a vested interest in keeping the world fat, unhealthy and in need of medication.

If anything, socialist systems such as the ones in France and Canada are worse. With 100% coverage (or close to it) for pharmaceuticals, France, where I grew up, is filled with self-medicating hypochondriacs, all in horrible shape. The French "pharmacies", with the staff in smart, white frocks and the clean, well-lit displays are a model for peddling medications people don't need as a form of quasi-entertainment. Inevitably, these establishments will come to the US and further intoxicate our pill-popping culture.

The reality is that few people need the kind of pills doctors prescribe for them. They need to eat healthier and move around more until they can hit their target weight.

Voodoo Medicine

As mentioned above, I consider "alternative medicine" to be worse than prescribed medicine – if that is even possible.

Since the dawning of the "New Age" movement, a number of fraudulent "healers", "reflexologists", "Chinese herb doctors", "crystal therapists", "acupuncturists" and the like are pushing "treatments" which would make the charlatan "elixir" doctors of the Wild West look like devout Buddhist monks.

Make no mistake: there is zero evidence that any of this stuff actually works. The argument of the New Age crowd is that the drug companies are conspiring to hide evidence. While I wouldn't put it beyond drug companies to do so, any logical person would agree that it's highly unlikely. But trying to reason with these people is like talking to those who believed that 9/11 was a big US government conspiracy, or that aliens are being held in the middle of Area 52. It's quite hopeless.

One of the more recent twists in New Age "alternative medicine" circles is the focus on "alkaline water" as a solution to all problems. Based on the idea that "acidity" is the source of all evil, and armed with PH paper strips to measure the acidity in your drinking water and urine, peddlers of this half-baked theory have turned it into a real, multi-level marketing enterprise, with an army of door-to-door salesmen pushing water "purifiers" that make your tap water taste like baking soda. Needless to say, none of this has any verifiable benefit.

SMOKING

Smoking is right behind obesity as the number one worldwide fitness problem. Let's face it: if you are smoking, you really can't do any kind of exercise in any meaningful way. Let's skip the fact that you have a pretty decent chance of acquiring lung cancer. Your main day-to-day problem is that smoking will make you lethargic, out of breath, and will poison your independent thought process to the point where an hour without a cigarette is unbearable.

As an ex-smoker, I can tell you that stopping is easier than both stopping drinking and losing weight. After a mere month, you simply don't need cigarettes. Just like drinking, my advice is to go completely cold turkey – just stop smoking and stay stopped. You may want to do this first before trying my method of stopping drinking, as the psychological pressure of doing both together may be too much. But in any case, you really need to stop smoking completely *before* you cut alcohol or drugs out of your life.

If you are still smoking and saying to yourself that you will quit someday, take a look at the picture below.

Figure 3 Smoker's lungs. A great reminder of what an awful habit it is.

The lungs on the right are your lungs – black and contaminated like those of a coal miner in 19th century England. Can you really claim that you are at all serious about your health?

Don't think for a minute that the damage smoking does to your lungs, teeth and brain are even remotely "OK". And yet, doctors will be happy to treat you for whatever problems you have, giving little more than a slight warning that you should stop smoking.

Cigars, by the way, are just as bad, if not worse. My father-in-law contracted throat cancer from his daily cigar habit. No matter how well the "cigar aficionado" lifestyle is romanticized in magazines and films, this is just another variant of nicotine addiction, with all the negative consequences.

GETTING WITH THE PROGRAM

The purpose of this chapter was to set the tone for a rigorous program that you should follow in conjunction with your non-drinking. The next two chapters go over what exactly you need to do: diet and exercise.

[6]

Change Your Diet!

WHAT YOU EAT is the single most important factor – far more meaningful than exercise – in how much weight you will lose. The great thing is that, in conjunction with stopping drinking, a simple, common-sense diet will work wonders on your body -- and it will do so very quickly.

When you cut through the clutter, you can summarize what is known on the subject in 7 basic rules:

Rule 1: Clean Out Your Fridge

Rule 2: Eat Mainly Fruits and Vegetables

Rule 3: Watch Your Carbs

Rule 4: Cut Out Fatty Foods

Rule 5: If It's Not Fresh, Avoid It

Rule 6: Write It Down

Rule 7: Step Outside of Your Comfort Zone

Let's go over each of these diet rules in more detail.

RULE 1: CLEAN OUT YOUR FRIDGE

A friend of mine (my AA sponsor) works a lot with overweight people as part of a "swat team" to help them lose weight. The first thing he does is he goes into their homes and starts throwing things out of their refrigerators.

Starting right now, take a close look at your refrigerator. You need to get rid of the following things IMMEDIATELY:

- Jars of mayonnaise
- Pre-made salad dressings
- Bars of butter
- Any leftovers
- Your entire collection of 2-year-old hot sauces
- Every single thing in your freezer – you don't need any of it

Your refrigerator should look completely pristine. We're going to replace everything in there with fresh fruits and vegetables, a few pre-cooked grains, a few (very few) pieces of lean meat and fish – and nothing else. And we are going to keep it that way.

Rule 2: Eat Mainly Fruits and Vegetables

The single best piece of advice that anybody can give you on a diet -- and the only advice that everybody can agree on -- is to eat mainly fruits and vegetables. That doesn't mean you need to be vegan or even vegetarian; it just means you shouldn't include a lot of meat, or even fish, as a large percentage of your overall diet.

This is a tough rule to follow, and requires some education. Most people are completely clueless in the fruit and vegetable aisle of the supermarket. The reality is that even if you are eating out, it's not all that hard to pick the vegetarian option. When you are at a steakhouse, pick a small fish plate and a big salad. When eating sushi, pick sashimi and go for the seaweed salad and the pickled vegetables. When eating Indian, go for the vegetarian curry. When eating Chinese, go for the sautéed mixed vegetables. At home, make broccoli, kale or salad a main course one meal out of two.

As long as you eat mainly fruits and vegetables, the quantity of food you eat really doesn't matter. You can eat an entire bag of carrots and only add 100 calories. You can eat as much salad as you want as long as you keep the dressing down to a few tablespoons of whatever you want.

RULE 3: WATCH YOUR CARBS

Zero-carb diets like the Atkins diet made waves throughout the 1990's when proponents encouraged people to eat as much fat as they wanted, but avoid carbs at all costs. Well, they were half right. Pasta made from enriched flour, bakery items, rice and desserts have almost zero nutritional value, and should be avoided -- except in really small quantities.

That doesn't mean you should eat tons of fried eggs and red meat. Which brings us to our next rule:

RULE 4: CUT OUT FATTY FOODS

Your body metabolizes fat almost instantly and turns it into fat on your body. One book I read made the point that animal fat goes directly from "your lips to your hips" in as little 6 hours. If you eat a fatty pork chop, for example, the fat cells from the chop can be found just hours later in your thighs.

Chemically, animal fats are known as "triglycerides" and look like this:

Figure 4 A triglyceride molecule. It looks like the letter E.

In this diagram, the red molecules are oxygen, the core black molecules are carbon (the "skeleton"), and the white molecules are hydrogen.

The triglycerides in the pork fat you are eating are very close in composition to your own body fat and are easily metabolized. Your stomach and liver don't even need to break them down; they can just conveniently relocate from the hips of the pig to *your* hips.

Genetically we are all predisposed to liking fatty food. The reason is that fat is an excellent device for storing energy. In fact, as my friend, the physicist Richard Muller, has pointed out, animal fat is 8 times better than TNT at storing energy. It's right up there with gasoline.

Your genetic forefathers either had a gene to like fat – or they perished. Think about it. 10,000 years ago, the instinct to eat the fat of a dead animal along with the taste for fat was critical to survival. Over time, this appreciation for triglycerides was encoded in the genetic material and passed down to modern man.

Unfortunately, now, in an era of ubiquitous fast food, this instinct is no longer helpful. On the contrary, our genes are leading us in the wrong direction -- towards a fat catastrophe.

This is one of many examples where, contrary to what Sheryl Crow said in her song, something can make you happy and really be very, very bad!

"IF IT MAKES YOU HAPPY, IT CAN'T BE THAT BAD" –
Sheryl Crow

Getting your advice from pop stars like Sheryl Crow or
Britney Spears is generally a very dangerous idea.

Fatty foods, drugs, alcohol and even smoking
all make you happy – at least for a while. And they all
are very, very bad for you.

On a pure calorie count basis, which is the
single most important factor for whether you gain or
lose weight, fats are the worst offenders. They are so
high in calories that just a tiny portion can completely
put you over the edge. For example, a single
tablespoon of salad dressing contains 60 to 80
calories. If you go to the average salad bar, the

dressing is served in ladles that contain at least 8 tablespoons. Welcome to a "healthy" salad with more calories in it than a Big Mac.

Cutting fats out of your diet is critical if you want to lose weight, and really isn't all that difficult. Here's a simple list of guidelines:

- Never, ever, use mayonnaise
- Don't reach for the butter at restaurants
- Go slow with salad dressings
- Always order leaner cuts of meat
- If you do love cheese (I do), keep the portions down

RULE 4: IF IT'S NOT FRESH, AVOID IT

Grocery stores today – even so-called "organic stores" such as Whole Foods -- are filled with dietary landmines. In fact, other than the fruit and vegetable aisle and the meat and fish departments, you can safely avoid 80% of what these stores are selling.

In particular:

- Canned foods are completely unnecessary. Why would you eat canned vegetables (or even worse, meat) when you can have the real thing?
- Prepared foods are often very deceiving. How much butter or fat is in that ready-to-go chicken cacciatore? You have no idea.
- Many large supermarkets have gigantic "olive bars". Olives are extremely high in fat and calories and should be avoided.
- Cheese is bad for you. Full stop. Yes, the enormous cheese aisle at Whole Foods looks "regional" and "fresh", but you shouldn't be making a visit there every time you go grocery shopping.

It goes without saying that you should *never, ever* eat junk food. Not only is it high in calories and low in nutrition, it will give you a "food rush" that is the exact opposite of the "slow and steady" approach that I am advocating.

RULE 5: WRITE IT DOWN

In Chapter 3, I encouraged you to keep a daily diary of your "transformation" through sobriety and health. Either in that diary, or in a separate program such as Lose It or FitBit, I also encourage you to write down what you eat and drink.

Being completely honest with yourself is the key here. Remember: nobody is looking at that diary except you, so there is no reason whatsoever to lie. Alcoholics are notorious for lying to themselves; they "remember" having just "a few drinks" when they really had many more. The same is true for writing down calories. You might be tempted to clock your salad at 2 tablespoons of dressing, but deep down, you know that it was four. Put down four.

If you count calories, and eat less than 1,500 calories a day, you *will* lose weight, typically around a pound a week. As I mentioned many times here, it's important to only focus on the new *low measurements*, because your actual weight can shift dramatically from day to day, and that could merely mean that you have a lot of water in your system.

In the next chapter, "Being Aware", I talk a lot about the non-physical (or what some people call "spiritual") aspects of being more aware or "in touch" with the world you live in. But without skipping ahead, there are lessons here for the physical side of existence as well. Eating right means first and foremost being aware of *what* you are eating and *how you look.* Take a really hard look at yourself, day after day and write it down -- especially if you deviate from your program (and you will!)

If you find yourself shoving a piece of cheese in your mouth, or a slice of pizza, or reaching for the butter tray or the jar of mayonnaise, take stock.

RULE 6: STEP OUTSIDE OF YOUR COMFORT ZONE

The pop artist Andy Warhol had a specific kind of diet. When at a restaurant, he would always order the food he disliked the most. That way, he was sure not to overeat. If you have seen a picture of Andy, while not healthy, he certainly wasn't overweight.

I think there is some truth to the "Andy Warhol" diet. By default, we all have some very bad things on our list of favorite foods. In my case, it's rib-eye steaks, cheese and saucisson sec (salami). Left to my own instincts, I would pick these over whitefish and grilled vegetables any day.

You really need to step back and say to yourself, "Yes, I love that, but it's just not good for me". Try something that you *think* you don't like, and try it with an open mind. You will almost certainly be surprised.

And first impressions are often not good indicators. It can take many attempts to correct an ingrained predilection towards unhealthy foods. Think of it as reversing bad programming on a computer. You may have gotten some of the bugs out, but there can still be major flaws left in the system.

A specific example in my case was breakfast. I went from alternating between no breakfast (not good for you, as you tend to overcompensate at lunch) to over-the-top breakfasts like eggs benedict, huevos rancheros etc. I was mentally aware that I should be eating a piece of fruit or a yogurt instead, but the few times I actually tried doing that did not feel particularly satisfying. It took several weeks of forcing myself to change my habits. Now there is nothing more that I like in the morning than a few berries and granola.

If you have a dog, you know how quickly the dog can get spoiled on a bad food diet. Just like you, the dog prefers high fat foods at every single meal in the day. And just like you, after a longstanding diet of fat and carbs, the dog will turn its nose up at a leaner, healthier formula.

It might help you plan your food intake to visualize that you are in fact "feeding a dog", or at least a different person than yourself. Push your own thoughts of what you *think* you like outside of the equation and try to just plan a good, healthy set of meals for that other "you" that you are now taking care of.

THE BAD FOOD "CULTURE"

Just as alcohol has ingrained itself in society and wormed its way into every aspect of contemporary life, the culture of fat and excessive carbs is likewise ubiquitous.

Let's start with the glorification of "celebrity chefs", and the notion that being a "foodie" is a desirable quality. Beginning with Julia Child in the 1960's, a new role model was created: the food-loving, calories-be-damned, bon vivant. Is it healthy? Who cares! The objective is to make a great hollandaise sauce, or a butter and wine reduction or a beef and bone marrow combination.

Julia Child and her progeny created a pantheon of "food gods" to emulate. Bored with France? Mario Batali, an overweight New Yorker with vague Italian heritage has cornered the market on how to "eat like an Italian". Wolfgang Puck, the

Austrian entrepreneur, has, unbelievably, made German food attractive. Bobby Flay, the Brooklyn homeboy, will teach you proper grilling technique. Emeril Lagasse owns the Cajun franchise. Anthony Bourdain is the specialist in grubby street food. The list goes on and on.

On the restaurant front, the rating system of the Michelin Guide, created in the '60's and copied by Gault et Millau, Zagat and others, defined a new set of *quantitative objectives* for foodie globetrotters. "How many three-star restaurants have *you* been to? How many have you been to in Barcelona? Have you tried Masa in New York? Zagat gives it a perfect 20". And so on.

It's easy to romanticize food, and especially unhealthy, fatty food, because our bodies are predisposed to liking it. Add a charismatic spokesperson like Bobby Flay or Rachael Ray, and it makes you want to immediately start cooking, or eating, or both.

For the first time in history, and for the vast majority of the general population, food has become a type of entertainment. What to do on the weekend? See a movie? Or better yet, go to a new restaurant. Traveling abroad? Let's plan the trip around some culinary destinations. Want to relax and get inspired? Flip on the Food Channel, or start browsing food blogs. And make sure to share every meal on Facebook or other social media platform.

We've gotten to the point where eating a simple, healthy meal is just not viewed as acceptable. Everything needs to be overly complex, rare, "worth the experience." (As I write this from the middle of France, the local restaurant here is now proudly serving kangaroo steaks smothered in rich, high calorie sauce.)

The lesson to learn from this is to not get swayed by these false gods. If you want to *look like* Mario Batali, then *eat like* Mario Batali, or eat at his restaurants. Watching the Food Channel, or celebrity cooking matches is a really bad idea for developing a healthy lifestyle. Just like Robert Parker romanticized wine, making us all believe we were missing out on life by not experiencing the mythical 1947 Chateau Cheval Blanc, these made-for-TV personalities are creating food myths to fill our dreams.

So forget molecular cooking, food safaris, timed food competitions, survivor-style cooking elimination rounds, and all of that nonsense. At the end of the day, you should be eating mainly grilled or broiled vegetables and a little bit of lean meat and fish. End of story.

[6]

Exercise!

THE NUMBER ONE problem most people have is extra weight. For this, diet (and in particular reducing calorie intake) is 80% of the solution. The other 20% is exercise.

If all exercise did, however, was add 20% to the impact of a diet, there would seem to be little point to it. There are, however, some other key benefits:

- Exercise clears your mind and stop you from mentally obsessing about the next drink

- Exercise relaxes you and makes you feel more grounded; it gets you more focused on your physical reality

For these reasons, I think it's very helpful to start a simple, low-stress exercise program in conjunction with stopping drinking and going on a diet.

Your number one goal (at least for the first 6 months) should be cardio. You want to get your heart rate up and accelerate your breathing (remember from the previous chapter that breathing is *how* you lose weight). In general, you just want to move around a lot.

Pedometers like FitBit, Jawbone Up, Nike Fuel Band and even the iPhone 5s Pedometer app are all systems that can easily tell you how much movement you are performing in a day. Whether you are running, walking or swimming, you can think of it as an equivalent number of "steps". You need to be taking at least 5,000 steps a day with a 10,000-step target.

PERSONAL TRAINERS

If you can afford it, there is nothing like a personal trainer for motivation. Not all trainers are created equal, but a good one will work with you to achieve your fitness goals.

If you are like the average overweight American, I would recommend making your entire initial goal *weight loss*. Trainers will tend to focus on machines and muscle building because they feel more useful setting and resetting the machines as opposed to cheering you on as you clock your miles on the treadmill, but the reality is most people don't need to work on their strength right off the bat.

GROUP EXERCISE

Much more affordable than personal trainers, group exercise classes (yoga, step, spin classes) are a great alternative for the recovering alcoholic. Not only do you meet more fit, healthy people than you would in a dingy AA meeting, you will also benefit from the upbeat, up-tempo coaching and music (in the case of spin classes) or calming meditative music (in yoga classes). Either way, it's a great way to get out of your head and into your body.

WALKING

My favorite type of exercise is simply walking. If you have a dog, you have an excuse to walk everywhere, meet other dog owners and stop and smell the roses. So, get a dog. Or just walk on your own, with headphones and an iPod if you want to add music to your experience. An hour-long stroll will get you 3 miles – or about 7,000 steps – which is just about

what you need in an average day without ever
breaking a sweat.

THE MEDICAL BENEFITS OF EXERCISE

Besides helping you simply burn calories,
exercise has been shown recently to have measurable
benefits on your health. It is strongly implicated in
fighting against heart disease, heart failure, strokes
and diabetes. The study, which was recently covered in
the New York Times
(http://well.blogs.nytimes.com/2013/12/11/exercise-as-potent-medicine/?_r=0), involved over 300,000
participants, most of whom received drugs. 14,000 of
them, however, merely exercised and took no drugs to
fight the same diseases. The conclusion showed that
exercise was at least as good as all known drugs in
fighting these diseases.

If exercise can have such measurable benefits
in the case of heart disease, it seems very likely that it

could have a vast number of additional benefits that we simply don't know about yet. And it stands to reason that it should: our bodies, which have evolved genetically over hundreds of thousands of years, are optimized for a strenuous physical existence. Just like a car left to sit idle in a garage will deteriorate, an unused body, engineered to walk ten miles a day or more, creates all kind of problems.

Well, that more or less covers what I want to say about the body. Let's now move to the equally interesting (and potentially more complex) subject: the mind.

[7]

Become Aware!

I THOUGHT OF CALLING this chapter "spiritual transformation", but as I discuss below, the mere mention of the word "spiritual" makes me cringe. And yet, as part of "my program" I definitely think you will either voluntarily or involuntarily achieve a complete change in your worldview, which AA refers to as a "(spiritual) awakening".

If you had asked me two years ago what religion or spirituality could possibly have to do with stopping drinking, I would have said, *"Nothing"*. Today, I have a different opinion, and yet I am still an atheist. Let me explain.

Regardless of whether or not you believe in God, if you drink a lot, you are in a very unnatural psychological condition. As I explained in Chapter 3, it is as if a virus has taken over your brain – a virus that is systematically wiping out all your problems (temporarily), making you feel invulnerable, all-powerful and completely self-obsessed. You are, in a word, *unaware*.

In a state of drunkenness, or even in between binges (as your mind is subconsciously pining for the next drink), you become completely oblivious to other people and your surroundings. It is as if you are sleepwalking. You're moving, but you barely avoid the obstacles in front of you, unaware of what you look like, and completely unaware of others.

This attitude will keep you drinking.

All it will take is one bad moment – a bill that you didn't expect, rejection from a date, a problem at work – and your mind will revert to the "I am all-powerful and I deserve a drink" mentality.

It's also why "white-knuckling" it, without a fundamental psychological shift, doesn't work. Stopping drinking is not about self-control; it's about rearranging your priorities and finding a different path in life.

Achieving a higher level of awareness in your life will not only give you a much better shot at not returning to the bottle, it will make you a happier individual.

If you are just beginning your transformation, I think it might be a good time to write out on a piece of paper the things that make you happy. I remember doing this in my "old life" and coming up with a list along these lines:

- Enjoying a good drink with friends
- Enjoying a great meal
- Achieving financial success

Interestingly enough, "a great relationship with my wife", "great, lasting friends", "giving back to the community", "helping others", or "being a decent human being" were never even considered. In fact, all three of my happiness "triggers" were directly related to alcohol.

- The "friends" part was just an excuse. Socializing with others was really just about drinking.

- The very concept of "meals" for me implied drinking. Food was only there to accompany wine.

- Financial success meant continuing my current state indefinitely without change, i.e., more drinking!

After listening to hundreds of stories in AA, I can tell you that my worldview was not only far from unique, it was almost textbook identical to that of every other man in the program.

This brings us to the God question. As a core part of AA, you are asked to "believe in a power greater than yourself" to "restore your sanity". This euphemism for God (and I do believe it is a euphemism, as the founders of AA were definitely Christians), really is all about redirecting your focus from your alcoholic self towards God.

If you aren't convinced, consider AA's Step 4: "We made a decision to turn our will and our lives over to the care of God as we understand Him". In other words, ask God to lead you to brighter pastures. You can scratch your head all you want, but AA definitely asks you to become religious.

Now, historically this certainly has something to do with the success of AA. Clearly alcoholics are a messed up bunch of people who can't think straight for themselves, and saying that you should "turn your will over to God" is really another way of saying, "don't trust your mind. You have been corrupted by a type of virus".

Now, as you do stop drinking – at least in my case – a remarkable transformation can occur. As you move away from the alcoholic ego-driven personality, you suddenly tend to feel much more at peace with the rest of the world and the other people in it. Random strangers seem much more interesting to you. Their problems become problems you can relate to. A strange serenity can overcome you in AA meetings, or outside of them -- a serenity that was completely absent from your former life.

This "connection" with the rest of the world can be a very intense, deep feeling. I believe that I felt this at my first AA meeting, and, from what I can tell, it is exactly the kind of "spiritual awakening" that religious people feel. In my case, however, I didn't feel in any way connected to a "higher power", a Christian all-powerful God-like entity or even some strange ghost-like "energy". What I was feeling was a heightened sense of being. I felt calm, reflective, and very, very real.

Deep Awareness

The kind of connection I felt is commonly referred to as "spirituality". I think it's a terrible term, because it implies that there is something different than the physical world out there. I believe that what I was experiencing was exactly the same real world that we all live in, but that I was just feeling life more deeply. I was not encountering any "spirits," just reality, but a reality perceived on a much more intense and meaningful level.

When you are in this calm, meditative state, you can feel the world move around you like water washing over the shore. You have a sense of your own breathing, you can feel the energy of the people around you, and regardless of who those people are, you feel a deep sense of community and love.

I'll call this state simply, "deep awareness". You need to be very relaxed and detached in order to perceive it, and it's difficult to maintain for long periods of time, as your brain will always revert to trying to solve the day's problems very quickly.

I want to pause for a second here to make a big disclaimer that I am NOT a card-carrying member of the "New Age" movement any more than I am a follower of Christianity or any other religion. I am just talking about a mental state that is achievable, with practice, and that is clearly associated with the right side of your brain (the center of creativity).

In his simple but effective bestseller, *The Power of Now*, the writer Eckhart Tolle focuses on attaining this awareness as a "guide to spiritual enlightenment". Eckhart has an interesting story: at age 29, after a long period of near-suicidal depression, he had an epiphany. "I woke up and everything was so peaceful. The peace was there because there was no self. Just a sense of presence or 'beingness' -- just observing and watching".

The addict or alcoholic (or even the chronic cigarette smoker) has very little chance of achieving any form of deep awareness. Minutes after finishing one drink, the alcoholic brain is busy figuring out how to get a second one, and a third, and a fourth.

Cigarettes focus the brain with a nicotine rush that appears to "clarify" things, but very soon after finishing one cigarette, the brain is busy subconsciously looking for the next one. No time to sit back and take stock of the world.

In his book, *Ecology of the Mind*, the anthropologist Gregory Bateson adds another angle to this discussion. Not only are we becoming aware of the world on a different level, we are becoming aware of our human "tribe" on a different level. Let me try to explain. We are not only individual creatures, but we also exist in a number of different group settings, such as within our families, our circle of friends, and our team of coworkers. Part of our programing is to function as a group member and not as an individual. Being able to get in touch with that "group dynamic" feels very "spiritual" and "deep". But it's not so much a unification with an external "God" as it is a unification with the other "cells" that make up the "human tribe" we live in.

As one human being to another, if you haven't experienced the kind of awareness I am referring to, don't despair. As AA says, quoting William James, "These spiritual experiences are of the educational variety". But like all other experiences, they can fade, and can easily be replaced by the normal, mundane feelings of jealousy, pettiness, greed, etc. (the biblical sins).

THE HUMAN CONDITION

Awareness and a deeper acceptance of the human condition are what get you through sobriety. You need something to compensate for the "on-demand" delusion produced by alcohol that you are the Master of the Universe. That something is usually expressed in AA meetings as the general feeling that no matter what happens, it's really going to be "okay". 99 times out of 100, our problems are completely imaginary: the money that we think we need would just end up spent on things that don't add any benefit to our lives; the person we are obsessing about could just as easily be ignored; and so on.

We criticize teenagers for being far too emotional about what other kids say to them in school, but we adults are also easily tricked into being too obsessed with money, our jobs, and how our peers perceive us. We need to step back and take a really honest look at our own shortcomings. (AA mandates that we actually take inventory of our flaws. This seems excessive to me, but it might be beneficial for some).

At the end of the day, sober or not, we are all going to get old and die. It's a hard fact of life, but from the point of view of evolution, it is a benefit for our species. And even if aging could somehow be arrested or reversed (which may or may not be possible in the next several hundred years), the universe itself operates on a cosmic scale that cares little about the individual inhabitants of our planet. Sooner or later, the sun will burn out, the universe will expand, and everything will cease to be. Even individual atoms – the core components of all matter in the universe – are thought to have finite lifespans.

Separated by trillions of miles from the nearest star, we live on the only planet in our solar system that can sustain human life. In other words, Earth is all we have. It's pretty remarkable, and we should nourish and cherish our home with all our energy. Our predicament is so crazy and random that we should just laugh and enjoy it instead of drowning out our worries with alcohol, cigarettes and suicidal thoughts like some French existentialist.

Quantum Mechanics

Since we are on the subject of the "Big Picture", and because it's a subject I know a fair amount about, I would like to bring up the subject of quantum mechanics, modern physics and cosmology.

Incredibly, over the last 30 years, astronomy, and specifically cosmology, has made huge leaps forward. Back in 1975, when I was in high school, the "Big Bang Theory" was still considered "just a theory". Now, a multitude of empirical evidence has confirmed it as fact, beyond a shadow of a doubt.

There are lots of great books and videos on the subject, but I highly recommend my friend Richard Muller's *Physics for Future Presidents* as a starting point. I also suggest all of Leonard Susskind's videos on YouTube.

A word of caution, however. Many accounts of modern physics pushed by the "New Age" movement are downright false. For example, just because the Heisenberg uncertainty principle says that if you observe a particle, you change it, does not mean you can "manipulate things" using the power of your thoughts.

It's also the case that many of the more modern theories of physics, such as string theory, are just that – theories. Nobody knows for sure if strings exist. In fact, if you read Lee Smolin's captivating books, there is a case to be made that the theory is intrinsically flawed in that it can, by definition, predict nothing.

After spending hundreds of hours actually working through the math of relativity and quantum mechanics, the main conclusion I can share with the reader is that reality is far more complex and strange than you can possibly imagine, and that any attempt to "grasp" what these equations mean by "analogy" is almost certainly wrong.

[8]

Get Organized!

TWO OF THE SIMPLIST and most overlooked tools for recovery are organization and cleanliness. In one of his many excellent books on Zen Buddhism, Alan Watts recalls asking his Zen master where to begin his path to enlightenment. He was handed a broom and told, "Sweep."

As addicts and alcoholics, and as citizens of the 21ˢᵗ century in general, we generally live in a disorganized, random fashion. We don't spend enough time looking at our surroundings or looking at ourselves in the mirror. Instead, we spend our time on email, social networks, mobile phones, or we're parked, vegetable-like, in front of TV and movies, ingesting vast quantities of meaningless information.

If you really plan on changing your entire life, which is what quitting drinking and getting fit involves, you are unlikely to succeed if you start from a state of disorganization.

I highly recommend that you spend a good weekend going through your closet, cleaning up your house, reorganizing your files and cleaning up your computer before you even start on the program outlined in this book. Trust me. It will make a big difference.

YOUR PHYSICAL APPEARANCE

The first place to start your 'cleanup' is with your physical appearance. If you are like I was, you don't find it enjoyable to look at yourself in the mirror. The person you think of yourself as, the person you once were, no longer matches the person you see every morning when you wake up.

The solution is not to ignore the mirror. On the contrary, you should take a really good look at yourself, and take a couple of "selfie" photo shots from your mobile phone. Better yet, ask a friend to candidly shoot some pictures of you before you even start on this program.

Obviously, a lot of change in your appearance will have to do with weight. As you lose 20, 30 or 40 pounds, you will shock yourself with just how good you start to look. No cosmetic surgery will be necessary; no lap bands or other procedures; just good, old dieting and exercise.

But there is more to attend to than just your weight. In particular, alcohol and stress show up as circles under the eyes, black marks, pale coloring and other, extremely unattractive traits. Take a good look at yourself and take notes. A lot of these things will change in just a few months if you stick with the program.

There are a few things you can start working on immediately. Treat yourself to a good haircut. Then go get a facial or a pedicure. Relax with a few good massages. Pamper yourself with a day spa – or better yet, take a full weekend off at a spa retreat.

These simple steps will start the process of getting you back into your body, and comfortable with who you are and who you want to be. Again, remember that this is just for you. No need to tell a single other person about it. Just start taking care of your own body, and appreciate it.

YOUR CLOTHES

We all have lots of clothes we no longer wear. In some rare cases, there are items in our closets that we forgot about and that we will wear again someday. But in general, let's face it: there is a reason we no longer wear those clothes. It's time for a change. Make a big pile of everything you haven't worn for the last 90 days, and head straight to the Goodwill. You are better off with less, not more, in your closet.

Now that you have disposed of your really hideous clothing choices, let's go through the rest of your wardrobe and throw out another 50%. Anything that is loose, old, in poor condition, or damaged should also go to the Goodwill or straight into the trash. As you lose 20 pounds or more, most of the items will no longer fit you anyways and will have to be tossed. You might as well start now.

From here, over the next 90 days, I want you to start buying some new clothes as you lose weight. Reward yourself by going on mini-shopping sprees; and don't wait until you hit your absolute target weight. So what if the tight jeans you buy after losing 10 pounds will seem loose after losing 30? It doesn't matter. You can always take them in. This is not about cost; it's about something far more valuable. It's about *you!*

I am also a big fan of spending a bit of money on a few good items of clothes – especially for guys. It's too easy for some of us to ignore ourselves, and focus exclusively on other people, or just on things that help us "fit in." My recommendation is to develop your own sense of style. Decide what you really like, and spend the money to get a few things that make you really feel good.

Late-night AA meetings are filled with younger people, and almost all of them dress in torn jeans, lopsided hats, badly-fitting tee shirts etc. Very often these same people seem confused that they are having problems finding jobs, and sticking to a sobriety program.

I have news for them. It's a tough, competitive world and it's only getting tougher. Not only are you competing with other clean, sober, well put-together individuals entering the labor force, but you are also competing in a global economy where internet workers from China, India and Eastern Europe are only a click away. You need every weapon you can get.

One thing I highly recommend as a general "organizational principle" is to make a list of every clothing item you own. Take a picture of the item, and inventory it in my Mozart app (www.mozart.co).

Being able to go over your wardrobe *virtually*, and decide how to prune it or add to it is extremely useful.

YOUR LIVING ENVIRONMENT

As a successful guy, I had a full-time, live-in maid who cleaned up after me six days a week. This was a huge mistake. It led me to become completely careless with my surroundings. I typically dropped my clothes anywhere in the room I happened to be prior to calling it a night; I left plates of food to stand without even bringing them to the sink; I often forgot to brush my own teeth.

Cleaning up after yourself is not a chore; it's one of the most important aspects of developing an awareness of who you are as an individual. You can still employ a cleaning person (I do), but you should generally run a tight ship with regards to both your living environment and your personal hygiene.

Not only should you keep a clean living environment, I recommend taking a fresh look at some of your design choices. Is the poster on the wall in your bedroom something that you really like? Or was it just there before you moved in? Do you really love that couch in your living room, or is it just something you live with?

Living with *your* design choices as opposed to somebody else's, or choices that were formed by accident (random accumulations of "souvenirs" for instance), can help you build *your* inner space.

Your Financial Environment

Like it or not, we all have bills to pay and obligations to meet. You can either deal with them head on in an honest fashion, or you can live in a state of denial.

My strong advice is to pay your bills immediately as they come and don't let things pile up. I had a friend who once stopped opening his mail. He figured the IRS would not care that he didn't file his taxes. He was wrong. It did take the IRS two years to catch on to his negligence, but they ended up getting back interest at mafia-style rates, garnishing his wages, and making his life an absolute hell for several years. As a result, my friend gained 40 pounds, became completely depressed, and ended up (sadly) committing suicide.

In many cases, your bills are too high simply because you are living beyond your means. It's worth spending some time alone or with a trusted friend going through your finances, and doing some basic planning. As much as you think you need a lot of things you have, you may very well *not*. Warren Buffet and I both drive older cars (mine is a 2002). I love the fact that I drive the same car I bought 12 years ago. It runs well and it looks good. Why should I change it?

Your Work Environment

The same cleanliness standards that apply at home apply at work as well. Keep your desk as clean as you possibly can (mine is absolutely pristine). File any piece of paper immediately, or deal with it immediately.

You will be more productive. Your coworkers/boss will appreciate you more. You will advance professionally and make more money. It's that simple.

Your Virtual Environment

These days, computers have replaced filing cabinets, agendas, calendars and paper organizing systems. It's possible, and I believe highly beneficial, to be as neat and organized in your online/computer world as you are in your physical one.

A few things that I have found that work for me may very well work for you:

- Use Dropbox or Google Drive to organize and store all your computer files on the cloud. You don't want to lose files just because you lose or damage your computer, or because you change laptops.
- Keep an absolutely clean desktop. Files on your desktop are, by definition, not on Google Drive or Dropbox. So get rid of them, or move them onto the cloud before you close your computer.
- Use point cloud systems like FitBit for your exercise records, Xero for your accounting, or my own system, Mozart.co, to save your posts and pictures. Nothing should be saved on your computer that is not somewhere else on the cloud.

- Keep a personal diary on Mozart or some other personal blogging platform. Microsoft Word works as well, but is not recommended.
- Use an online calendar that syncs to the cloud like iCal/iCloud or Google Calendar.

SIMPLIFY

If I had to summarize this chapter in a single word it would be: *Simplify*. Simplify your wardrobe: eliminate the clothes that you don't wear, and any ones that don't make you feel great. Simplify your financial situation: pay your bills immediately and keep a clean financial slate. Simplify the environment around you. Reduce clutter. Go for less decoration, not more. And simplify your virtual life. Keep tidy records of everything you own, every plan you have, everything you have to do.

[9]

Actually Do It!

THE PURPOSE OF THIS BOOK is to affect change. I don't want to merely *tell* you about the amazing transformation that I went through; I want you to *actually experience* it, directly, yourself. It really *is* possible. No matter how stuck you feel in your old habits, no matter how hard it seems to lose weight and get fit, complete physical and mental transformation is not only possible, but it can happen much faster than you think.

In this chapter, I put together all the previous elements presented into a program that you can follow, step by step. I want to give you a basic roadmap of what to expect and when. And I want to give you the kind of coaching that will lead you to decisively conquer what is arguably the most insidious, complex and devastating virus that has ever challenged mankind: alcohol.

DAY 0. PREPARATION.

Before the Allies invaded Normandy on June 6, 1944, six months were spent preparing the attack. Multiple landing beaches were considered, the size of the German defenses were estimated using a variety of intelligence sources, and a detailed attack plan was put in place with estimates for losses and casualties. Before a single GI had landed in Omaha Beach, General Eisenhower and his staff had a good idea of what they were up against, how long it was going to take, and exactly how hard it was going to be.

Going into battle with alcohol, and trying to achieve the kind of transformation we are talking about here, requires a similar type of planning and preparation. You aren't just going to take a body that is used to getting a third of its calories from ethanol, and a mind that has been conditioned to always be looking for its next drink, to a completely new level without resistance.

The first thing is simply to assess the situation.

- How much are you *realistically* drinking every day?
- How overweight are you?
- What does your everyday diet look like?
- How much exercise do you *actually* do every week?
- Are you really ready to go into battle?

Let's go over each of these, one by one.

HOW MUCH ARE YOU REALISTICALLY DRINKING EVERY DAY?

If you drink over a glass of alcohol a day, in my book you are an alcoholic. The word may sound a bit harsh, but it's accurate. It essentially means that you feel a compulsive need to drink each and every day. It means that without alcohol in your system, you will feel uneasy, edgy, and uncomfortable. If you drink a bottle of wine or the equivalent (4 beers, 3 strong drinks), you are definitely, 100%, physically addicted to alcohol. You may think of yourself as a "social drinker" (a category on many dating sites), but the reality is that you are really a garden-variety drunk. You are getting a third or a fourth of your overall calories from alcohol and it is going to be very, very tough to quit.

If you drink substantially more than a bottle a day, you are going to need to medically detox, under supervision, before you really attempt to stop drinking. Chronic abusers can ingest incredible quantities of ethanol. For example, one woman I met in AA was drinking half a gallon of vodka a day. Another man was buying Xanax pills in 5,000-pill bags, and consuming dozens daily, mixed with six or seven shots of vodka. If you think your habit can't degenerate to these levels, think again.

So the first thing is to accurately assess, for yourself only, exactly how much you are drinking. Make sure to include every single drink, and count double shots and "generous" pours as two drinks, not one. Don't lie to yourself. It will get you absolutely nowhere.

HOW OVERWEIGHT ARE YOU?

Your weight varies every day. That's normal, as you eat and drink various amounts, and your stomach is either fairly full, or empty. But weigh yourself every day for a week, and take the lowest of those seven readings. Now, take a look at the "ideal weight" online. (There are many formulas for what's ideal. Pick one in the middle of the pack). The difference between your reading and the online number is the measure of how overweight you are.

It will seem like a lot. In my case, I was convinced my "normal weight" was 185 pounds, simply because that is the number to which, all other things equal, I seemed to revert. My ideal weight is about 160 pounds, so I was a full 25 pounds overweight.

Take stock of this number. In general, you aren't going to lose much more than a pound or a pound and half at most, per week. Losing 25 pounds will take you about 25 weeks, or about 6 months. Losing 50 pounds is likely to take you a year. There simply isn't any great way to accelerate this; you are dealing with the laws of physics (in particular, the law of energy conservation).

The point is, weight loss is a marathon, not a sprint. And you need to train like a marathoner, not a sprinter. It's not about going to the gym for two hours and trying to burn it out on the treadmill. It's not about going on some all-protein diet, or picking only foods in a certain food group. It's about cutting back your overall calorie consumption by about a fourth, reducing your intake of fatty foods and carbs, and eating more vegetables.

WHAT DOES YOUR EVERYDAY DIET LOOK LIKE?

As I have mentioned repeatedly, it's critical to write things down. Before you even start your transformation, it's a good idea to get a baseline of what you are currently eating.

Using a tool such as LoseIt or FitBit, religiously record everything that you eat or drink for 7 days. Are you eating meat once a day? Twice a day? Let the data be the judge. Record how much butter, mayonnaise, sauces, and salad dressings you help yourself to on your own. And then get a total daily calorie count. That's what we have to work with.

HOW MUCH EXERCISE DO YOU ACTUALLY DO EVERY WEEK?

You probably know if you go to the gym (or not) every week, and how many times. But unless you have a pedometer like FitBit, Jawbone, or Nike Fuel Band, you most likely don't know how many total steps you are taking every day, including walking from your car to your job, climbing stairs etc. These devices are phenomenal for excavating that kind of information.

As I discussed earlier, I don't believe that exercise is the key to losing weight; diet and not drinking are. But fitness still plays a vital role in your well being. Simply walking for 45 minutes a day will have an amazing impact on how you feel, and, all things equal, will burn about 200 calories a day, or a third of a pound of fat per week.

ARE YOU REALLY READY TO GO INTO BATTLE?

Sun Tzu, the Chinese military strategist, said that all battles are won or lost before they are started. As I have said repeatedly, this battle is going to the hardest one you will ever fight. Much harder than stopping smoking. Much harder than any professional accomplishment that you have ever fought for.

If you don't see yourself as the alcoholic that you are, you have very little chance of beating alcoholism. If you don't think of yourself as overweight – despite what all the charts, tables and medical assessments show – you simply won't lose weight. And if you think fitness is for other people, not you, guess what: you will be right.

As an interlude, a friend of mine is advising a client who has a serious alcohol problem. According to the man's doctor, his addiction could be life-threatening unless brought under control. When confronted with the idea that the solution might be to stop drinking, the man declared, "Life is too short and I like drinking. Find another solution".

What the man can't see is that, while he likes drinking now, he actually would not miss it if he stopped for even 3 months. Accepting the possibility that you actually *can change* is half the battle. Whatever you are thinking now, accept for a moment that you are very possibly under the influence of a strong addiction – a virus – and that your thinking itself is not clear, or in your best interest.

One thing you should *not focus on* is the notion of stopping drinking forever. It's very easy for the alcoholic mind to reject the idea of never having another drink on the grounds that 'life is too short', and that lifelong sobriety too big of a decision. On the contrary, your goal should be to stop for a month and then reassess. Once you hit that 30-day mark, set your sights on 90 days. Once you hit 90 days, focus on six months. This war is fought one battle at a time.

It's also a personal war. Drinking alcohol is so socially acceptable that you are constantly exposed to it. You need to expect temptation and more temptation. Your friends will drink in front of you. At restaurants, the first question is usually, "What kind of drink would you like?" On airplanes, and in airport lounges, free booze is the norm. In hotels, your room will typically come with a stocked mini-bar. At the grocery store where you shop, a huge liquor and wine department will tempt you.

In these kinds of environments, it's vital that you talk to other people who have successfully stopped drinking. Reading books like this is generally not enough. That is why I highly recommend that you check out AA. With a few caveats, it's an excellent program.

THE FIRST 90 DAYS

For most people, the physical cravings of alcohol last about 90 days. It could be earlier, and could be significantly later, but 90 days seems to be about the average.

The first thing to do when you stop drinking is to really get a handle on your sobriety date. Commit that date to permanent memory and enter it any number of "sobriety calculators" available for your iPhone or Android that will tell you how long you have been sober. It's all about calculating days from that point on, and celebrating every milestone that you achieve.

In your first week of stopping drinking, I highly recommend checking into an AA group in your neighborhood. There are meetings going on everywhere, at all times of the day. Regardless of your schedule, you can easily fit a one-hour AA meeting into your life three or four times a week. (The recommended regimen is 90 meetings in 90 days, but I can't say I've achieved anything close to that attendance record, nor do I think it's entirely necessary for all people).

Not only should you join AA, you should get a sponsor. A sponsor is nothing more or less than an AA member who has gone through the program and can coach you through it. Amazingly, it's a completely free-of-charge service, something you might otherwise spend hundreds of dollars a month on, or more. The "viral nature" of AA is that members become sponsors, who bring in new members and so on, all with almost no money changing hands.

On the subject of finances, however, I would recommend, spending the money and allocating the time for a ten-day or two-week detox program/retreat without work, bad food, or other distractions. I recognize that these can be expensive, but you should ask yourself how much you would pay to actually lose 20 or 30 pounds. For most people the answer is, a lot. I guarantee that you will enjoy your newfound health far more than that new car, addition to your house or shopping spree at the mall.

Within 90 days, if you stick to a reasonable diet, exercise two or three times a week and cut out drinking altogether, you will almost certainly lose 15 pounds. That alone will make you feel like a different person. The alcohol cravings will miraculously disappear, and you will find yourself adjusting to the new, healthier you.

90 Days to 6 Months

Once you hit the 90-day mark, the conflict with alcohol takes a different shape. You no longer feel the daily physical cravings rampant during the first phase of your addiction recovery program. Life settles into a new normal as you adjust to a better, healthier way of being.

During this phase, your focus should be to set the foundations for a new, long-term life plan.

Eliminate toxic people from your life

One of the realities of stopping drinking is that you will lose some friends, and gain a lot of new ones. Unfortunately, many of the people that you hung out with in your old life will not be sympathetic or encouraging at all when they hear you are cleaning up. Their reaction will be to feel threatened, or at least uncomfortable around you. Rather than deal with them, it is best that you step away and cease all contact. The last thing you want is to be invited to a party or an event where a lot of drinking is taking place.

The reverse of that is you should actively seek out non-drinkers and include them in your new social life. If you are single, look to date another sober person, or at least one who truly only drinks "socially" (unlike 90% of people on dating sites who classify themselves that way). Make friends in AA and open yourself up to the many sober people who will approach you once they realize that you are now "one of them". I guarantee you that they are out there.

DEVELOP A CLEAN, SOBER, AND FIT LIFESTYLE

Once you hit the 90-day mark, you can really work on developing a clean lifestyle that fits your schedule and environmental constraints.

Organize your week. Set specific exercise goals (for example, two visits to the gym and a yoga class), and specific weight loss goals (lose a pound a week on average). Write everything down. Keep a diary on Microsoft Word, or on my web-publishing platform Mozart.co, and keep track of your diet and exercise on FitBit.

Clean yourself up. Throw out old clothes that no longer fit, and buy a few new ones at 90 days, and more new ones at 180 days. Make that your reward for losing the weight. New clothes also will make you feel better. This is all about a new beginning, and it should start with your wardrobe. You don't need to spend a lot of money; just get clothes that fit, and feel good.

Dropping clothes sizes is an incredibly rewarding thing. In my case, I went from a tight size 36 waist to a size 30 in 180 days. My casual shirt size went from XL to Medium. The pleasure of buying new jeans and polo shirts in the smaller size still puts a grin on my face. And there is nothing more attractive than a slim, fit person. It has a far greater impact on how you look than any amount of money you can spend on designer clothes.

Besides clothes, a lot can be said for better general standards of cleanliness. Most alcoholics, and really a great portion of the everyday population, live in a disheveled, untidy fashion. As my yoga teacher Pretzel in San Francisco used to say, "You should do everything very deliberately, like it counts." That includes keeping your car, your desk and yourself as clean as you can. You will find that simply cleaning up your mess – and cleaning it up yourself – is incredibly therapeutic.

You will also learn to adapt your life to fit a new, sober lifestyle. When at a bar, order a soda water with lime, or have the bartender make you a non-alcoholic cocktail. There are many that are absolutely delicious: virgin margaritas, virgin pina-coladas, virgin mojitos and so on. Sugar-free red bull, while not strictly recommended, is preferable to alcohol if you really want to "spice it up."

When traveling, ask the hotel to remove all alcohol from the mini-bar before you arrive. Look into getting a trainer to meet you at your hotel and go for a run in the park or exercise at the hotel gym. Make the gym or the pool a factor in choosing one hotel over another, not simply the "star rating" or the guest rating from an average (probably alcoholic) reviewer.

And, most importantly, don't stop going to AA meetings. The biggest factor in relapse is forgetting about the program and your commitment to stop drinking. Don't let time trick you into thinking you are "cured." As they say, "Nobody ever graduates from AA." Once an alcoholic, always an alcoholic. Between your genetic footprint, which is likely alcohol-prone, and the mental pathways that have been imprinted in your brain, you will never have "a clean start."

REPLACE TOXIC CULTURAL INFLUENCES

If you step back from the chaos of modern life, and the self-centered craze that is the alcoholic and addict's world, you also begin to notice the toxic cultural "noise" of modern life: meaningless television shows, talk radio that is talk for talk's sake, assembly-line pornography, and music that might make sense "under the influence", but seems dry and monotonous when viewed from a sober perspective. I will leave it to you to identify which of these corrosive elements to say goodbye to. There are so many better ways to spend your time.

If you haven't already done so, I would start by getting rid of your television set. As Steve Jobs himself said, television is an incredibly corrosive and addictive thing, because the focal point of your home ends up in an "always on" state. In addition, they are generally ugly devices. I would only rate video game consoles, where the goal is to kill virtual people, worse, in terms of the impact on the brain.

Ten years ago, it was very hard to imagine the typical house without a television. TV's, like hardline phones, seemed indispensible. Today both are obsolete. While computers can also be highly addictive, at least they don't pollute the common living space's audio and visual environment. And they are getting more interactive. The web is no longer about "surfing websites"; it's about communicating with other people. And that's generally a good idea.

Travel is always a great idea, and with cheap flights, you can now go almost anywhere on the planet from anywhere else in just 24 hours. Take a friend, or just go on your own. There is so much to discover. In the last 6 months I personally went to Alaska, Chile, Argentina and Fiji. Bhutan, Vietnam and the Iceland are on my "to do list". Just thinking about them makes me smile.

Classic movies are available essentially for free, courtesy of Netflix, and almost every piece of music known to man is available for streaming on Spotify. If you want to increase your knowledge, the world's best universities, including my alma mater Stanford, now offer phenomenal continuing education videos on iTunes, all completely free of charge. YouTube has phenomenal music instruction videos on piano, guitar and other instruments. Even sheet music can be downloaded from Scribd.com for just a nominal rate.

The modern world doesn't have to be toxic. It is only so because we let it be so. And we do it mainly out of ignorance. As Plato describes in his allegory of the "cave", we are looking at shadows against a wall, thinking this is all there is to life. Real knowledge is about understanding what is making the shadows.

Nobody has an excuse to live a miserable, toxic life. If you clean up your act, and start by eliminating the bad, the good will come in by osmosis.

[10]

AA

A BOOK ON HOW to stop drinking by an Alcoholics Anonymous member needs to say something about the organization that is AA.

I want to be 100% clear that I am absolutely recommending you make AA one of the cornerstones of your transformation program. As I mentioned in Chapter 4, just talking to sober people repeatedly is the best way to stay sober. And sober people, for lack of a better place, hang out at AA.

But AA, to the rest of the world, seems like a mysterious organization, with bizarre cult-like characteristics, like the Masons, or the Church of Scientology. Look on the web, and no amount of Google searches will give you a good idea of what to expect when you walk into your first meeting. Will you be converted to a new religion? Will you be forced to hang out in a raincoat in front of a church drinking coffee and smoking packs of cigarettes? Is there chanting involved?

For the benefit of AA, which because of its decentralized nature can't properly explain itself, I will give it a go.

AA was founded in the 1930's by a man named Bill Wilson, shortened in AA-speak to Bill W by a convention invented to protect the reputation of recovering alcoholics. Bill W and his friend Bob S took some of the ideas of an earlier alcohol recovery program called the "Oxford Group" and baked them into the movement that is now Alcoholics Anonymous.

The movement has its own book called, *The Big Book*, written in 1939 by Bill W, with passages by Bob and recovery stories of 20 other alcoholics from the era. It's an excellent book, and although a bit dated, it still reads very well and is downright funny at times. You can read it for free online, or pick up a complementary copy at any AA meeting.

Unlike almost any organization that I am aware of, AA is completely decentralized, meaning there is no central head office responsible for the kinds of things head offices tend to be responsible for – raising money, charging people, setting rules and so on. Instead, anybody can start their very own "AA meeting" anywhere they want, just copying the format of any other AA meeting, and adding any kind of twist they want.

The AA book, *The Twelve Traditions* sets some guidelines as to how these meetings should be run. In particular, the founders of AA realized early on that the system needed to be self-supporting as opposed to accepting donations, or charging dues. What that means in practice is that people pass around a basket at meetings, and everybody contributes a few dollars to cover the cost of renting the meeting space.

Meetings are generally one hour long and typically consist of one or two designated speakers who share their recovery stories, followed by a sequence of shares from the rest of the people at the meeting. People may raise their hands to talk, the meeting may go round robin ("everybody shares"), or sometimes the speaker alone will choose which individuals share.

A number of people are in charge of running the meeting. These rotating, voluntary "commitments" include a "timer" who is responsible for making sure people don't go on for more than their allotted minute or two, a "literature person" responsible for distributing *Big Books* and other brochures, a person in charge of cleanup and so on.

Other than the *Big Book* itself, (which was started by practicing Christians and which heavily pushes the reader to "turn himself/herself over to God"), and a few prayers during the actual meeting, it's not a religious organization. It's also very different from a cult, as there is no leader, no dues, and no brainwashing.

The program is highly successful. Just in Los Angeles, on a given night, there are close to a thousand meetings ranging in size from 5 to 250 people. There are iPhone apps to find meetings, and you can easily read the *Big Book* on your phone to receive daily words of AA wisdom.

As you go through the program, you will find some meetings and people that you like more than others. But, regardless of where you are, you can be pretty much guaranteed there is some meeting happening today – and probably right now -- very close to you.

AA also utilizes the concept of "sponsors". These are folks who have been through the program, are sober, and who help others get sober. I have a sponsor, Frank, who has been a huge help to me, especially during the first months when I was still having strong cravings for alcohol. You can easily find (or replace) your sponsor at any AA meeting.

AA makes use of "12 steps" or guiding principals of the program as set forth by Bill W and the other founders. You will generally meet with your sponsor about once a week to do "step work". This means going over these 12 steps again and again and discussing how they apply to you. This is where it gets a bit "cultish" and "scientology-like", as your sponsor is going to want to drill in the principals of the *Big Book* as if they came from the 21st century Bible.

The system works well when it works, but people definitely do relapse. However, in the AA literature, there is a phrase that is repeated over and over again that says, "Rarely have we seen a person fail that has thoroughly followed these simple steps". One of the steps is not drinking, so by definition, "that simple step" will keep you sober!

Because AA is almost completely decentralized, there is no central "design team" responsible for building the AA website, and so the AA website sucks. The meeting finders tend to be primitive and are rarely updated correctly, which can be confusing for first-timers. There is no universal social network for getting in touch with other AA members, so people hand out phone numbers and you end up getting a lot of text messages in the beginning resembling this:

415 677 1221 – "Great seeing you at the pier meeting. Call me. Sam."

That's great, except when you can't figure out who "Sam" is. A Facebook-style photo would have been quite useful. And many times the name is omitted, and you don't have the person in your contacts, so the text ends up being,

310 781 7784 – "We're getting together at Café Zero at 8 if you want to join."

Fascinating, except now you are not even sure if it's AA-related, let alone of the identity of the person who sent the text.

If my Mozart.co project takes off, and if I can convince enough people in the LA AA community to use it in a private setting (the anonymity/privacy angle is key), maybe I can help move this texting system into the 21st century.

Notes

CHAPTER 1

HEARTBREAK RIDGE

I realize that my opening salvo may seem a bit rough to some of you – especially fragile "AA newcomers" who are just looking for a helping hand. Unfortunately, my best advice is the kind of tough love given out by Clint Eastwood as the drill sergeant at the beginning of "Heartbreak Ridge".

For reference, the scene starts like this:

"My name is Gunnery Sergeant Highway and I've drunk more beer and pissed more blood, banged more quiff and busted more ass, than all you numbnuts put together... I'm here to tell you that life as you knew it has ended. You all may as well go into town tonight. You may as well laugh and make fools out of yourselves. Rub your pathetic little peckers against your homies or stick it in a knothole in the fence, but whatever it is, get rid of it. Because at 0600 tomorrow your ass is mine."

The YouTube video can be found here:

http://www.youtube.com/watch?v=6uvF-emJDSI

ON HOW BEING HEAVY OR LEAN SHAPES YOUR VIEW OF EXERCISE

A recent study published in the New York Times (http://well.blogs.nytimes.com/2014/01/08/how-body-size-shapes-our-view-of-exercise/?_r=0) sheds some light on how overweight people perceive exercise. Not surprisingly, there is a direct correlation between how thin you and how fit you are, and whether or not you perceive exercise as "fun".

The study concludes:

Such data might at first seem discouraging, underscoring the possibility that being obese or overweight is self-reinforcing, although it is impossible to know from this study whether a dislike of exercise contributed to or resulted from weight gain.

I can help the authors and answer the question: "both". Being overweight makes you dislike the very concept of exercise, as it is easier and preferable not to move around with the extra fat you are carrying as "baggage". It also contributes to further obesity, as you will do less and less to shed the extra pounds.

This type of vicious cycle, where a bad habit creates further, self-reinforcing bad habits is what addiction and abuse is all about. It's also an interplay of physical bad habits (eating too much, drinking, not exercising) and mental bad habits (feeling too self-centered, being mentally sloppy, abusing other people). This is why I think a complete change is the only way to go.

CHAPTER 2

LETTER TO MY FIRST WIFE

In addition to my gushing post on Facebook, I penned the following letter to my first ex wife (who I was married to from ages 25 to 32). It's pretty amazing that I came to this level of self-realization so quickly. Most people, unfortunately, don't.

Hi Louise.

This is a going to be a long letter, and I apologize for its wordiness. I want to make amends for my behavior during our marriage and state that I am, and have always been, an alcoholic. This self-destructive behavior started very early in my life. I don't remember certain details now, and would be very thankful if you could help me fill in some of the blanks. I apologize for everything from the bottom of my heart.

And now on with the letter!

I went to my first AA meeting two days ago. Going into that meeting, I had very low expectations. Clearly I was not a drunk. Sure, I enjoyed social drinking, and yes, I had a real interest (let's call it a hobby) in fine wine, especially French wine. But I was not, by any stretch of the imagination, an alcoholic.

I was also certainly not a religious person. I laughed at religion; I admired the works of atheists like Richard Dawkins, and I cringed whenever I heard the word "spiritual". I knew that AA was somehow connected to all of that, which made me loathe walking into that meeting.

For the last thirty years, my path was a very self-directed, self-assured one that clearly was the superior one. Look what I had achieved! Company after company. Success after success. And there was alcohol, always by my side, a partner in this success.

Looking back, a few moments stand out as representing the pinnacle of this delirium. I remember around 1990, when I first became wealthy (at age 30), that I started really collecting and drinking wine. What a great hobby! The fact that I knew all the names of the French Grands Crus Bordeaux and could discuss the subtleties of the year 1985 in Burgundy clearly was a phenomenal badge of achievement. So much so that one day, going over my growing wine collection, I realized that I now had amassed over 2,500 bottles – more than one for every weekend probably left in my life. Now the amazing thing was not that I was in the least concerned that there were only 2,500 weekends left (50 more years multiplied by 50 weeks per year); it was that there were not enough occasions to drink more fine wine! I would have to start drinking 100 bottles of wine on Saturday *and* Sunday for the rest of my life to burn through my collection! How depressing!

The second moment that stands out for me was around August 1993, when you first joined AA. I believe that we had actually gotten our divorce by then (maybe you can remember the actual date). But the key thing was my thought at that time: "Wow. That is so bizarre. I didn't even realize that Louise drank. She must be very lonely and lost and must need some bogus spiritual excuse to cope with life. What a poor woman! Not like me, with my new software startup well on its way, and all my money in the bank (a lot for the time, compared to anyone else I knew)."

Anyways, I apologize again. I know now how absurd this thinking was.

The third moment was sometime in 1995 or 1996, when I was now a bachelor living in San Francisco. My house, which was one of the nicest and most prestigious ones in the entire city, was a monument to all I had achieved. My new friends, who were all younger than me, congregated around this house, and Fred, the eccentric millionaire. And as always, alcohol was my steady companion. The night that really stands out is a crazy party that I hosted where I knew maybe 10% of the people in my own house. There were hundreds of bottles of wine; I probably drank three or four bottles myself that night. I remember being dragged into a closet by a girl (not my girlfriend), and discovering that she had taken a lot of my furniture when I finally woke up at 3pm the next day. But of course, I had no idea that I had a drinking problem.

The fourth moment was around 2005 in Austin, Texas while visiting some kind of redneck classic car show. I was now remarried to my current (soon to be ex) wife, and living in Los Angeles. We had befriended a country music band called, "Ryan Bingham and the Dead Horses". Ten years had passed since the party in San Francisco and I had managed three more glorious financial exits. I was sitting talking to one of the musicians, and I remember telling him and the rest of the band, while drinking straight tequila out of a bottle, that I was, "quite possibly the smartest guy in the world". And I believed it. That night I got so drunk that I managed to destroy an entire hotel room, black out and not even remember exactly how it happened the next day. The hotel sent me a bill for several thousand dollars.

In all of these instances, I was rejoicing over my incredible success and how amazing my life was. Clearly such success deserved nothing but the finest French wines, great 18-year-old single malt scotch, 50-year-old Armagnac, etc. And as always, this was completely destructive to everybody closely around me: you, my girlfriends when I was single, and my second wife, Anouk. There was a clear correlation between these peaks of alcohol consumption and my belief that I had achieved almost "god-like" qualities, and that other people should be lucky enough to be with such an amazing person, period.

And then came my AA meeting. I walked into that meeting extremely casually, thinking generally that this might be a good idea for the divorce process, and probably couldn't hurt. I vaguely acknowledged my drinking might have been somewhat excessive. I still had a bit of gout left in my left foot (in reality, this had become a regular and increasing problem. But more on that later).

I walked in and listened for 10 minutes. The only way I can describe what happened is to call it a religious experience. In just 10 minutes, I "got it". I understood completely that I was like these people, and I accepted that willpower would do me no good. And while I still have problems with the idea of "God", I felt in that moment a deep connection with the room and the energy and honesty of the people in it. I could not stop crying and wiping my tears. It just all made sense, all of it. And I made exactly the same vow that you made 20 years ago. I surrender to whatever you want to call it – God or a higher power – and pray that I can have the willingness to stay sober and make amends for all the self-destructive, and just plain destructive, behavior of my adult life.

That's the story so far. I am going to AA every day now. I am so happy that this organization exists. It is just phenomenal, and I think it will save my life.

Per Step 9, I am making amends to you, directly, for all the damage I have done to you over our years together. There were definitely some great times, but the damage caused by the drinking, and the delusions of grandeur and pompous behavior are just crystal clear to me now. For the first time, I completely understand why you divorced me, and I also understand why you yourself joined AA. I am so proud of you (and it brings tears to my eyes to tell you this right now). You are a great person, and so is my second wife, and alcohol ultimately was to blame for our disagreements.

Anyways, that's it. That's my story – what I remember of it. As I said earlier, I would be very thankful if you could help me remember more details of my drinking and excesses during our 7 years together. I want to understand exactly how bad it was. As an alcoholic, you by definition forget these things and focus on the "glory days" when you were consuming vast amounts of ethanol molecules – (C2H5OH) – the single molecule responsible for all this damage.

Anyways, with love, your friend for always, and deeply apologetic,

Fred

CHAPTER 4

THE MATH OF POPULATION GENETICS

I did a PhD in Applied Mathematics/Operations Research at Stanford University. One of the professors there was an amazing individual named Samuel Karlin. Karlin was more than just a superb mathematician. He decided mid-career that he wanted to rise to the top of the field of genetics as well -- and he did. Karlin's work on Markov models of population genetics is still viewed as the gold standard in this field.

For more information see

http://en.wikipedia.org/wiki/Samuel_Karlin. I am

sure a Karlin type approach to the math of addiction

growth would make a fine PhD thesis.

CHAPTER 5

THE PHYSICS OF WEIGHT LOSS

The fact that weight loss is entirely due to
breathing is a very poorly known fact that I learned
from my friend, the physicist Richard Muller. Muller
himself applied his physics knowledge to his own
weight loss and dropped 30 pounds.

A FAT TAX

I am not the first person to propose a fat tax.
The idea was proposed in 1942 by the psychologist A.J.

Carlesen, and was reintroduced in the 1970's and 1980's by Kelly Brownell at the Rudd Center for Food Policy and Obesity at Yale. While it has yet to be introduced as policy in the US, it is currently being considered in the UK under the government of David Cameron.

I've visited three detox centers over the last 8 years.

First and foremost, I've been to Lanserhof (www.Lanserhof.com) in Lans, Austria 5 times now. It is relatively expensive (initially about $7,000 for two weeks), but absolutely top notch in all regards. Lans (as it known in Europe), is really the premier detox destination for German speakers. They do speak English there, however, and Russian as well. But you won't necessarily be doing a lot of talking, as the 800-calorie daily diet, combined with the cleaning "bitter salts", makes you feel like you have just consumed a bottle of Drano.

In two weeks, you will lose about ten pounds. The majority of that will be water, which you will quickly put back on. But as far as a way to start on your path to a better you, it's the best money can buy.

Here in the US, we have the Canyon Ranch in Tucson, Arizona (www.canyonranch.com). The Canyon

Ranch is almost a high-end hotel with a touch of a focus on exercise and healthy living; it's not a true detox center. It can't really hurt you, but it will hurt your wallet. I find it very hard to recommend it to the reader of this book. Besides, the heat of the Arizona sun makes being outdoors unbearable most of the time, except for early in the morning or late at night.

I've also been to the Body Mind Restoration Retreat in Ithaca, NY (www.bodymindretreats.com). This is a wheatgrass-focused detox system that is built in an ancient hippie commune. It's perfect -- if eating dandelions for food and drinking copious quantities of foul-tasting wheatgrass is your thing. It certainly isn't my thing, and truth be told, I lasted exactly one day there. Complete waste of time and money! I should have known better, as I went to Cornell for undergraduate studies and I saw firsthand that Ithaca was one the places I needed to make sure I never visited again in this particular lifetime.

Overall, I will say that while a *one-time* detox is a great idea for recovering alcoholics or food addicts, it's not a permanent solution. A much better idea is to actually get in shape, and *stay* in shape. Subjecting your body to a continuous detox/retox cycle makes zero sense.

CHAPTER 6

THE ENERGY OF FAT

My friend Richard Muller, who has an excellent book and free video series out on YouTube called, *Physics for Future Presidents*, makes a great point that animal fat and gasoline are both far better places to store energy than even TNT. For example, a pound of animal fat has a specific energy of 37 (MJ/kg), while TNT only has a specific energy of 4.6. You can look this up yourself on Wikipedia at http://en.wikipedia.org/wiki/Energy_density.

CHAPTER 7

THE "NEW AGE" MOVEMENT

One of the more annoying things about the 21st century is the proliferation of vague, "New Age" thinking that has permeated our collective consciousness. This movement, however, is hardly new. In his excellent book, *Madame Blavatsky's Baboon*, Peter Washington traces the history of modern "spiritualism" back to a turn-of-the-century crackpot named Helena Blavatsky. Blavatsky and her entourage created the "Theosophical Society" in an attempt to fuse all religions together into a single, ill-conceived mishmash involving communication with the dead, a Far East element, and various other cult-like attributes.

(http://www.amazon.com/Madame-Blavatskys-Baboon-History-Spiritualism/dp/0805210245)

Eckhart Tolle

Tolle is one of the world's bestselling "New Age" authors. His book, *The Power of Now,* was promoted by Oprah Winfrey, making it an instant bestseller, and in the process, Tolle a de-facto multi-millionaire.

Despite having significantly more money at his disposal than his program of "just being" would seem to require, he still actively commercializes his teachings in the form of "Eckhart Tolle TV", a 6-month "Journey of Transformation" for the bargain price of $99.95.

That being said, his original book is genuine and worth reading. You can buy it from Amazon, or, of course, at http://www.eckharttolle.com.

QUANTUM MECHANICS

Max Planck, Bohr and Heidegger would be turning over in their graves if they had any idea that the complex, experimentally provable subject that they discovered -- quantum mechanics – had become the cornerstone of the New Age movement, used to back up any number of crackpot ideas.

The art-house movie, "What the Bleep", released in 2004, amplified a popular misconception that quantum mechanics implies that group consciousness can affect the material world. This flawed reasoning goes something like this: Since "observation" of a single particle can "affect" that particle, the same must be true in a "macro" sense. Nothing of the sort is true, of course. You can't cure cancer, for example, just by "thinking about it", or "rearrange your own DNA" just by intense concentration.

Unfortunately, quantum mechanics (like relativity) is a very difficult subject, and one that requires a modicum of mathematical knowledge in order to even begin to grasp it.

If you are actually up to spending the time and energy needed to gain an inkling about the subject, I recommend the videos of Leonard Susskind as the single best authoritative source. Susskind was one the fathers of string theory and all-around one of the most brilliant people alive today.

http://www.youtube.com/channel/HCz-bwdkPPVBs

These are difficult lectures to grasp, filled with lots of equations typically, but some of them are more general in nature. In any case, Susskind is the closest thing to Einstein that we have today, so it's great to just get a taste for advanced physics from the horse's mouth.

CHAPTER 8

PLATO

The allegory of the cave is from Plato's *Republic*. The entire text can be viewed online, for free, at http://classics.mit.edu/Plato/republic.html. Plato is, surprisingly, very easy to read and makes as much sense now as it did when it was written in 360BC.

ABOUT THE AUTHOR

Fred Krueger and his dog Alaska are active members of the Los Angeles tech ecosystem.

Fred has started 14 companies, exited 8, and is busy at work on 2. He maintains a blog at www.fredkrueger.org, which was created using his own web publishing tool

www.mozart.co

31458265R00118

Made in the USA
Lexington, KY
12 April 2014